P9-AEX-358

TO WRITERS, WITH LOVE

TO WRITERS, WITH LOVE

by Lesley Conger

Boston
THE WRITER, INC.
Publishers

Copyright © 1971

by

Lesley Conger

Library of Congress Catalog Card Number: 73-146550

International Standard Book Number: 0-87116-063-3

MANUFACTURED IN THE UNITED STATES OF AMERICA

Mus musculus
requiescat in pace
at your feet

Contents

Preface

WHEN I wrote my first few columns for *The Writer* half a dozen years ago, I thought, as each appeared, *Yes, this is all very well and good, but how can I go on, month after month?* Now I find myself wondering how I could ever possibly *stop*. If ever I do, it will be like breaking off a flourishing correspondence with a good friend. I expect it might hurt.

I was very happy with the decision to do this book, pulling some of the columns together in a more permanent form. After all, a book like this one has one overwhelming virtue: it's already written before you begin. But choosing forty columns to reprint wasn't the easy task I thought it was going to be. Some pieces my editor and I knew we couldn't leave out; letters from readers had told us, over the years, which ones those were. Others, mercifully few, we knew we certainly didn't want to put in — for the same reason. As for the rest, we read and reread, considered and reconsidered, and I hope we've chosen the best of them. We've tried.

Please note: this is not a How-To book, except maybe how-to-keep-going-when-you-feel-like-quitting. I'm not going to tell you about margin widths and return postage, or how to describe scenery, or how to plot. But you may find something in here that will tell you how to survive as a writer, as I have survived.

I am, I think, about as average a writer as you can find. I am not wildly successful (not yet!); but, working on an old portable typewriter at an old desk in an old house, usually wearing old jeans and a pair of grubby deck shoes, I've done a lot of writing over the past twenty years or so — fiction for magazines, plays for radio and television, two books for adults, two books for children. And these columns, the making of which I have enjoyed as much as any writing I have ever done.

For there is something very pleasant about addressing such a special readership. I have felt all along that I am writing to people I know. Letters from readers have told me how often we share the same enthusiasms, the same fantasies, the same frustrations, the same writer's block. We are, of course, not identical; but in a sense I can say, *I have met my reader, and he is me.*

TO WRITERS, WITH LOVE

1

To Writers, with Love: Here Is Your Gift

WE aren't strangers, you and I. For if you write, or want to write, I know you at least in some small measure — because I know myself. So I come to you as a friend; and I would like to come bearing a gift.

I've thought long and hard about it. A gift for a writer, I thought. But what you really need I can't give you, no more than anyone can give me what I really need: time, courage, endless patience, limitless energy.

A gift . . .

The word will begin to look silly in a minute, I thought, as any word does when you stare at it too long. And then it was as if I had picked the word up and turned it over in my hand, seeing another side to it. A gift is not only what you give people; it is what they have already. A gift for making friends . . . a gift for flower-arranging . . . .

And you — if you are, deep down, a writer (whether or not you have a long list of published writings makes no difference in this case) — you possess one of the greatest gifts in the world.

A gift for words?

No, not that.

Yours is the gift of being able to use your life at least twice over, once in the living and again in the creating.

3

Yours is the gift of being able to pour your life and your self into your work as few others are privileged to do. Every thought, passion, prejudice and passing fancy, all loves, fears, and memories — all are yours to take and shape and use, and in the using to know again.

You have the gift of making your life and your being into art, until you and your work are one. For the writer, there is nothing left out. There is no boundary between living and creating. A television repairman cannot pour his private dreams and visions into the tubes of your set; a heart surgeon must not let his unique view of reality and his secret fancies enter into a delicate valve operation; a pilot may feel totally alive only while flying, one with his machine in a mystical unity; yet there are whole areas of his experience that have no bearing on his flying and for safety's and efficiency's sake had best drop away from him once he leaves the ground. But a writer brings his complete personality and his entire life to his task. He can use, if he wishes, every experience he can recall, and some, indeed, beyond recall, that have marked and influenced him nonetheless.

The writer, despite the respect (with reservations and some suspicion) and the occasional financial rewards society offers him, lives — as do most artists of all kinds — on the fringes of our socio-economic system, not doing, in the view of many, any real share of the world's necessary labor. But he is more a whole man than many another because he does not have to be fragmented by his work. His work may take him now and then from his home and family, but it does not subtract him from himself. Where do you draw the line between Phyllis McGinley, wife and mother, and Phyllis McGinley, poet? Was there a real division between William Carlos Williams, poet, and William Carlos Williams, M.D.? Root out of James Baldwin's writing everything that depends on Baldwin's identity and life history, and what is left? It is the whole man who writes. A writer who is a father is a father as he writes, and because he is, it makes a difference. It matters that he loves his child so much that it hurts; it matters that he was born in Boston and raised in Albuquerque; it matters that he cannot stand caged birds or cut flowers, that he lost his mother when he was four and has a brother who excelled at everything (except words!), that he has one broken marriage behind him but great faith in the marriage that followed and still endures. It matters what books he read as a boy, what gardens and rooms and sleepy train rides and aged great-aunts he remembers, what sounds and smells and terrors are printed indelibly in his mind.

You may say, what I write is not so personal. Apart from suggesting that it may be more personal than you think, I answer: Then make it so — or at least part of it. Enter into your work more deeply; even a work of scholarship benefits immeasurably by having a discernible author, a personal style, evidences of an original mind at work. (Nothing can be quite so pallid, so unconvincing, so difficult to read as a scholarly work which appears to have been written by a computer!) As for me, I have written two books of a very personal sort, each one a kind of journal, but even in stories and plays which are basically fiction, my life and self have made their mark. Who else can take that particular Sunday drive of thirty years ago, that face seen yesterday on the street, that half-forgotten playmate, that sharply-remembered loneliness, and make it all into something that can cause a stranger a continent's breadth away to pause, recalling a long-ago loneliness of his own? Only I; and in some other case, only you.

Dear friend — enjoy your gift, and use it in good health.

2

Inspiration: It's Great When It Comes

EVEN if you firmly believe that inspiration is 90% perspiration (and I don't), that other 10% is still worth talking about, because it must be what makes all the difference. Man cannot create by sweat alone.

Let's abandon — before we even begin — any attempt to nail down a precise definition of inspiration or at least of that mysterious residue of inspiration that's left after the 90% has evaporated. Trying to define inspiration is as foolhardy as trying to define love, and worse than trying to catch a leprechaun with a torn butterfly net. The best we can do is to throw out a cordon of partial definitions and trust that somewhere inside we have trapped the elusive thing.

Writers use the word inspiration even more loosely than such a misty word deserves to be used. I've often reported having an *inspiration* for a story when what I really meant was that I had an *idea* for a story. For an inspiration is not merely an idea; you can have an idea for a story (or a poem, or whatever) which is far from inspired. My notebooks are full of such, dozens of them. You can write a story without inspiration, and it can be a competent, readable story that brings you a substantial check. I've done it. Most professional writers who need a steady income have done it.

But if "inspiration" isn't "idea," then what is it? I

think of it as a kind of illumination which may come along with an idea or may later light up an idea which has previously arrived uninspired. By its etymology, inspiration is *breathing in;* an idea which is inspired has had something breathed into it, transforming and enhancing it, bringing it to life. Often it seems as if you can *see* the inspired story whole, off in the distance — a mirage, glowing just above the horizon. All you need to do is to mount your fiery typewriter and gallop in that direction. Unfortunately, my choice of a mirage as a metaphor is too painfully accurate: Successful arrival is not assured, by any means.

Brewster Ghiselin speaks of the "unsearchable insight" which is inspiration; Stephen Spender talks of it as the beginning (and the end, as well) of a poem, and quotes Paul Valéry's phrase "une ligne donnée" — *a line given.* Unsearchable. Given. Such words cannot apply to the sweaty 90%, but they are the essence of the shy, fugitive remainder. You cannot really hunt for inspiration; it is a yearned-for but unexpected gift. Often, indeed, the *givenness* of inspiration is so striking that the receiver's second reaction (after delight) is suspicion: Can this really be meant for me or did I read it somewhere? Is it genius, or plagiarism? (Sometimes such suspicion is well-founded, alas! But our profession is fraught with hazards.)

It is only reasonable, therefore, that inspiration doesn't happen very often. Sometimes a succession of ideas will come to you charged with light. More frequently, you run across ideas, but all you can do with them is to jot them down — or, if you trust your memory, tuck them into a corner of your head — and hope that on some good tomorrow that special something will happen to them. This may not occur until years later — which is why I keep a notebook. To those who scoff at notebooks and say that any idea worth using will be remembered, I can reply only that while rereading old notebooks I have a number of times seen a forgotten, pedestrian idea suddenly lift from the page with luminous wings, and fly.

We have been talking about inspiration as a sort of radiance surrounding an idea; but it may also attach itself to the creator apart from any created work. For — and this is not as airy-fairy as it sounds — inspiration may arrive by itself without any central idea to make it immediately useful. Dorothy Canfield spoke of "a generally intensified emotional sensibility" and of "occasional hours or days of freshened emotional responses." In such a state, the writer is himself inspired (though inspired *to what* he does not know), and he may linger in this inspired, intoxicated condition for a long time without direction or objective, every nerve and sense tingling in an almost unbearable readiness.

I don't think there is much we can do to induce this exalted state in ourselves on order. Moreover, few of us could bear to remain so inspired for long. It is often as painful as it is exhilarating to be so naked to the world; a constant state of high inspiration would be a hair's breadth from madness.

Since you cannot search with certitude for inspiration but must instead be willing to take it gratefully as it is given, must you then sit idly and wait, perhaps forever and in vain? If I thought so, I'd drop the whole business and enroll in a course in hotel management or cost accounting. On the contrary, whimsical and unreliable as inspiration may be in its visitations, the waiting can be directed, purposeful, and consciously encouraging:

First: Suppose it's raining and you want to collect rainwater, so you go out with a ketchup bottle; you're not going to collect much. It's obvious you'd have more luck with a wide-mouthed jug or even a basin. Therefore, in the constant rain of ideas, impressions, sights, sounds, personalities, and happenings that you are being bombarded with (and you *are,* simply because you are alive and in a complex world), you cannot profitably wander about with your mind and senses constricted to the dimensions of a narrow bottleneck, or, as some people do, with an umbrella up. You must train yourself to be aware, conscious, observant, and at the same time wide open, almost indolently receptive. You must be a bowl or a sponge.

Second: Once you have an idea, you must not treat it with too much respect. Ideas should be picked up, turned inside out and over, twisted into new shapes; an idea should be regarded as modeling clay which has to be warmed in your hands before you can make anything out of it. This does not mean that you should sit stubbornly and viciously trying to shape a mass of cold, resistant material; but a playful and uninhibited touch is more likely to liberate that unsearchable insight, to flick the switch of that sudden illumination, than is a fearful and gingerly hand.

So: Be receptive, be playful; and finally — the absolute dictum on what to do until the inspiration comes: *Work.* You will work gladly with inspiration, but work calmly and steadily without inspiration if you must, so that when inspiration does arrive you will have developed the skill with which to bring it to your reader.

3

The Search for Perfect Working Conditions

I DO not know personally any wealthy, prolific, established writers — I do not ordinarily associate with other writers or indeed with anybody much; as the mother of seven children, my primary concern is to find solitude, not society — but I am certain that all wealthy, prolific, established writers have found that *sine qua non* of success, Perfect Working Conditions. Wealthy, prolific, established writers do not create their Nobel- and Pulitzer-Prize-winning works while a small girl prowls through their desk drawers, unrolls several miles of Scotch tape, and dumps boxes of paper clips on the floor. No; every wealthy, prolific, established writer writes in a quiet, restful, book-lined, leather-and-oak study, shut off from the rest of the house by doors too heavy to be opened by anyone under the age of eighteen. Or in the tower of a castle on the precipitous overhang of a rocky cliff at 10,000 feet altitude, served by a hardy, taciturn delivery man who weekly brings the groceries and mail, mainly checks, from the village below, negotiating a road passable otherwise only to snowmobiles or Sherpas with ropes and ice-axes. Or in a lighthouse. Or a firewatcher's lookout, during an exceptionally damp season.

(And now you know my private daydreams.)

I am, of course, still searching for perfect working conditions, which, I tell myself, is why — though I am

10

semi-established (by that I mean I have an agent and a publisher and barely enough income to give me unkind thoughts about the Bureau of Internal Revenue) — I am neither wealthy nor prolific. Give me perfect working conditions, I cry, and I will show you my literary heels!

Naturally, one writer's perfect working conditions may be another writer's nightmare. Once, for example, I spent fifteen months learning how to write when the sun was shining. No — I was never, except at the whim of infants, one of the Night People; but I was a lifelong resident of the foggy, drizzly, rainswept Northwest, and fog and rain and drizzle were my natural working environment. Then we moved to Nevada. Fog and rain and drizzle I could not get; in fifteen months I experienced about thirty of what I would call good working days. And yet there are writers, I kept telling myself during the long, bright, blazing, unproductive hours, who actually *deliberately* go to sunny Mexico to write! Incredible! Anyone knows that it is far easier to write on a nasty, wet, miserable day and that all writers should be sent to a colony I intend to establish in Forks, Washington, where it rains five days out of nine and 120 inches a year, and great works of literature can be produced by the bushel. Therefore, in the face of hard facts (Name a great writer from Forks, Washington!), let us grant the existence of idiosyncrasies. Each man's perfect working conditions are his own.

It used to be that every few Sundays, in our search for perfect working conditions, my husband and I indulged in a fury of furniture-moving. Pressured by a middle-sized home and a giant-sized family, we brought more and more work furniture into our bedroom, until at last the name *bedroom* was hardly applicable. There was, for one thing, no bed. But we kept some large chunks of foam rubber stacked up on the floor, and when late at night we began to fall over sideways at our desks, we shoved the furniture aside and spread these out to sleep on. There were advantages: no dust collected under the bed, and no doctor needed to prescribe a board under the mattress for any of *our* backaches. However, the situation was a few removes from ideal. My husband's work requires that he mumble and hawk away in an Indian dialect that sounds as if he has a small fishbone caught in his throat; he likes to work with the radio on, but cannot tolerate my spurts of typing. My work requires that I read dialogue aloud with feeling, get up and pace (where, on top of the furniture?), file my nails, bang erratically at the typewriter — and I must have absolute quiet to do it in, free of Indians, and especially free of the radio, which *I* cannot tolerate.

Over those crowded years, various solutions — short of infanticide, murder, divorce — suggested themselves. I have heard that noise should make no difference as long as it is noise about which you may remain unconcerned (unlike the noise of the refrigerator door opening, or the noise of sibling rivalry rising to massacre); true — and how I admire, for example, those writers who can write in cafés! But I never seem to get to a café, and besides I suspect that most café proprietors are too unsophisticated to want tables occupied for literary rather than dietary purposes, or mayhap too greedy. Numbers of books, I understand, have been written in public libraries, but the public libraries I know are places of teen-age rendezvous and thus no better than home. Again, one writer I have heard of writes in her car, another in her bathtub. But I am lucky to get near cars and bathtubs even when I want to go somewhere or to get clean; like the public library, cars and bathtubs of my acquaintance are full of teen-agers. So we solved nothing in those years. We simply endured — miracle enough.

Our house is larger now, and our family smaller; still I

continue dreaming about that quiet, book-lined study, that castle two miles in the air, that lighthouse, that lookout. But I long ago concluded, after losing the better part of fifteen months because of my addiction to fog and murk, that the worst idiosyncrasy a writer can have is a too-narrow definition of what constitutes perfect working conditions. For the truth is that the search for perfect working conditions — like the long wait for that golden Year Off — is in large measure a blind and a dodge, an excuse for lack of discipline and for failure to achieve the proper working conditions inside the skull.

But of course there are some tastes in perfect working conditions that simply cannot be relinquished. I once read that Truman Capote writes while lying down. Now there, I thought, is something I cannot do. I must be upright, in a chair at a desk; certainly not on a couch, absolutely not in a bed. So — one of the most productive weeks I ever had, a week during which I revised and typed the concluding sections of my second book to my almost complete satisfaction, was spent in a general hospital, where I worked propped uncomfortably in bed in a room facing west, in the dead of a hot summer, interrupted by thermometers, needles, bedpans, meals at insanely early hours, and visitors. I was, I am sure, the only mother in the maternity pavilion who had to rush to wash carbon smudges from her hands when the babies were brought in for meals. I had reached the point, in enthusiasm, in confidence, and in brute determination, at which working conditions no longer mattered. The real goal in the search for perfect working conditions is to reach that point — *and stay there.*

4

The Compulsive Writer

THE greatest pleasure I get out of my thoughts lies in putting them into words and putting the words to paper. This is a process so essential to me that I have trouble understanding how others can get through life happily without it. In the course of a day (any day, no matter how routine — and most days I do not even leave the house) — I find at least a dozen things to commit to paper: experiences, encounters with ideas while reading, observations on everything that surrounds me.

I am, then, a compulsive writer. And, like all compulsive writers (for I am sure I am not unique), I do not always wait a decent interval between an experience and the search for words in which to express it.

Decent is the word, I think. Consider a writer who has the ability to become detached even at the most deeply involved moment and to note to himself that here, in his own anguish or joy, in the exaltation or misery of those around him, is the germ of a story. Consider, to make it more concrete, the mother bending over the sickbed, the wife sharing a moment of despair, the sister shouldering burdens in a family crisis, the sympathetic, listening friend — each of them at that very instant composing sentences to nail the immediate experience down as a butterfly is pinned to a board. Surely anyone but another writer would find this not only indecent, but grisly and

14

cold-blooded. It makes of writers a loathsome breed, whose tender glances are suspect, whose tears smell of ink — in fact, a kind of bird of prey.

I myself am often struck with horror and suffused with guilt at the outrageous way in which I convert experience into material before it stops moving. But I cannot reform, for the compulsive writer is not satisfied merely to recollect in tranquillity and then transform recollection into art; he sees life as art, instantly, as it happens.

Luckily I have never had to justify this compulsive on-the-spot writing of mine to any non-writers, for nobody has ever caught me at it outright. There is, after all, no such thing as an instant story; there is instant perception and, to some extent, instant composition, but rarely, of course, anything approaching instant publication. This delay happily provides the decent interval which in the writer's mind does not exist. So, while people have on occasion seen (or thought they have seen, for they are quite often mistaken) the life sources of one of my stories, they have never been aware of the fact that the story was, to me, a story even when it happened. I'm not going to tell them, either. People, especially families, regard writers with enough suspicion as it is.

I must nevertheless contend with my own feelings of guilt. These overcome me most sharply and painfully when I am with family and friends, husband and children, and realize how they would look at me if they knew, indeed, how I had just been looking at them! And yet —

Unless all you ever write is a self-justifying autobiography, writing forces you to think even if only momentarily the thoughts of other people and to see through other eyes. I have written, for example, from the viewpoint of a young epileptic, an old Indian, a Catholic missionary, a 17th-century martyr, and the wife of a compulsive gambler.

These were, of course, complete imaginings; but I have also followed one of my own frequent suggestions to student writers, that is, that they attempt to write their own experiences from points of view other than their own, both as an exercise and as a way of opening up wider vistas on their material. You were wronged at some time in the past? — suffered from someone's ingratitude, perhaps? Tell about it, but from the opposite point of view. It cannot help but be salutary, like throwing open a window in a musty room.

In one of my stories, taken most directly, though not stenographically, from life, a young couple take their small children with them to clean out the summer cabin which they have had to sell in order to get cash for the down payment on a house. When I began writing the story, I knew only — as I had known when it happened — that this was surely a story; I did not know exactly how to treat it. I began writing it willy-nilly, just getting it down. "It's dark," says one of the children, when the cabin door swings open. The husband had forgotten how small the cabin was, and notes that it smells musty and sad. "It always was dark," the wife answers sharply, and I realized as I wrote it down that her (my) abrupt reply must have stung like a whip. "I hate to sell the place," the husband says quietly, a page later. The wife replies, "It's already sold." And at this moment in the writing, the wife in me winced, but the writer had a flash of recognition. *This* was the story: not the sad fact of selling the beloved cabin they had never really gotten around to using, but the sad lack of rapport — the husband tenderly examining old dreams, while the wife (because she could not bear it otherwise) remained unsentimental, curt, businesslike.

The story — and it had to be the husband's story — was painful to write, and yet, from the writer's point of view, easy, now that it had fallen into shape for me, now that I understood both my characters and their motivations, and knew why "they (we) had spent the whole day hurting each other."

Still, even if you do not shift your point of view, it is surely difficult, if not impossible, to make art out of experience without in some measure being forced to understand more of experience than your part in it. In the act of creation, you must, I think, see yourself as others see you — and see others with some of the tenderness you usually reserve for yourself.

But does this perception of life as art diminish the writer's emotional involvement in it *at the moment?* Does, then, the poet feel less deeply because he begins to make a poem of his feelings, and does the sculptor love less passionately because his beloved's form is sometimes bronze to his eyes or beneath his hand? These questions cannot be answered lightly. But if something is being sacrificed in this lack of a decent interval, it may be worth it, for the compulsive writer who is writing life on the spot may be moving not into a cold-blooded objectivity but toward that warm-blooded objectivity we call understanding. And this understanding, enriching the moment rather than impoverishing it (for it is, if anything, *more* involved and *less* detached than heedless, egocentric emotion), this the compulsive writer can transmit to others. Such is his job, his challenge — and a privilege.

5

The Desk-Drawer Syndrome

I HAVE been writing short stories and don't know what to do with them," writes a housewife in Ohio.

Don't know what to do with them? What on earth do you think you ought to do with them? Ship them to your Aunt Beulah, who used to teach English and coach girls' basketball in Bismarck, N.D.? Or roll them up and put them into bottles and float them out into Lake Erie?

But I don't say it, although — I might as well. Ah, the world is full to overflowing with would-be writers. And yet, not all of them are talentless; this I freely admit.

But, talent or no talent, most of them will never get anywhere.

Why? Why does talent lie neglected and unpublished? Because somebody never gave it a chance, that's why. And after years of reading letters from would-be writers and teaching creative writing to extension and night school classes, I know who that somebody is.

Would-be Writer, it's *you.*

For two years running, when I was full of fresh and naïve optimism, I issued a challenge to my writing students. In addition to manuscripts, I said, I would like by the end of the term to see a few rejection slips. I confess this at the risk of alienating all the editors of my acquaintance who may be horrified at the thought of being deluged with the impossible manuscripts of talentless neophytes. The risk is small — never mind, fellows — because in two years I did not see or even hear of a single slip. Yet each year I had several students with perceptible writing skill; each year I received several manuscripts which with some polishing and revision would not have raised howls of derision and groans of despair in the editorial offices of the appropriate magazines. Had they ever arrived, that is.

I have always answered my fan mail to the best of my ability and to the decimation of my limited writing hours. I am no critic, but I have given my opinion of manuscripts. I am no agent, but I have suggested possible markets. I have been a teacher and have done my best to direct what talent I have run across. And always, *always*, I wish the would-be writer luck and say, "Let me know how it goes." Do you see the mailman staggering up to my door, loaded down with progress reports? Actually, no; those are coupons worth 6¢ on new brands of detergents. I think that in the past several years I have received two letters from would-be's, letting me know. I could suppose that all the others have gone on to fame and fortune and have been so ungrateful as to refuse to let me know, but I know in my heart of hearts that what really happened was this: They read my letter of advice and criticism and then put their manuscripts back into their bottom desk drawers, where they lie to this day.

Sometimes would-be writers are simply lazy. When I have given hard-hitting advice on the amount of work necessary to develop an embryo talent, my correspondents have obviously taken one look, shuddered, and quit cold. In teaching writing, I have gone to great lengths to suggest stories, to outline further plot development for wispy beginnings, to delve into individual students' backgrounds for story material worth working on; I have written themes and one-sentence story synopses on the blackboard, have brought in newspaper clippings or other material which seemed to me to be stimulating and fertile. What happens? Roughly one would-be writer out of twenty will actually take up an idea and attempt to do something with it, while the rest just sit.

Well, the lazy ones have wasted my time (and theirs!), but let us leave them alone — as they deserve to be left. What about the others, the ones with some talent and at least one manuscript I deemed worthy of attention — what afflicts *them*?

It isn't sheer laziness; this is not what holds back the Ohio housewife with the already-written short stories she doesn't know what to do with. It isn't ignorance, either; for even after I tell her what to do with them, she still doesn't do it.

Perhaps her typewriter is in hock, and the post office is closed, and she's run out of paper — but if so, it all happened after she managed to get a letter off to me.

I know what it is. If I knew the Greek for "editor," I could coin a fancy word for it, ending in *-phobia*. It is, at any rate, what I sometimes call the desk-drawer syndrome, or, to be brutally outspoken, *cowardice*.

There are a few people who like to write totally and entirely for themselves, squirreling the pages away in some hiding place or other and never caring whether or not the glance of any other human eye ever falls upon them. But these are not the people who join writing classes, nor are they the ones who write appeals for literary assistance in the guise of fan mail. And I find it difficult to remain eternally tolerant of those who obviously aspire to be published and read and yet do all their writing for a desk drawer.

What are you cowardly would-be's afraid of? All an editor can do is to say *No;* nobody shoots you for trying.

Twenty-seven editors can say *No* without drawing blood once. And if you are afraid of discovering that you are no good, you can even console yourself by suspecting — or proclaiming loudly! — that all twenty-seven of them are wrong; it can happen. It hurts, of course it hurts, to see that Manila envelope coming back in your own horribly familiar handwriting, but it isn't fatal. And some day, instead of a cold, printed rejection slip clipped to the manuscript, there will be a letter telling you *Why* the editor is saying *No* and perhaps suggesting *How* to get him to change to *Yes;* and eventually, if you are not afraid to work, there will be no Manila envelope at all but only that long, delightfully thin one with the check inside, and you will have to look at your own handwriting only when you endorse it.

If you have talent, look around for the person who isn't giving that talent a chance. Try using a mirror.

And remember this: I have yet to meet an editor who goes about the country armed with a search warrant allowing him to prowl through would-be writers' desk drawers. For you, if you possess talent and a couple of completed manuscripts, the first step toward success may be a step in the direction of the post office.

6

A Quiet Book about Gorillas

WHENEVER I go to a library or a bookstore I am drawn to the books on writing, the books about writers, and to the books by writers writing about themselves and their work. Many of these turn out to be helpful, some nearly indispensable, and a few quite useless — but all of them are at first glance irresistible.

For I could spend all my reading time reading about writing and writers, as many a scholar, alas, spends all his reading time reading about his scholarly specialty. It is tempting, and never more tempting than at those times when my work is going badly. Then the desire to read still another book about writing becomes almost uncontrollable, like the desire of a hypochondriac to try still another kind of pill. At such (and frequent) times, I hate to pass up books on writing for fear I may miss something that will set me right.

But pass them up I do.

Obviously, I believe in books about writing or I wouldn't be writing this book. But in addition, I'd like to recommend to you the unexpected instruction you may find in books *not* on writing, and since I cannot predict what you will find, I shall have to give you a couple of examples of what I have found:

1. I was rough-drafting part of a projected book when I was overcome by the depressing notion that what I was

writing was too quiet and too contemplative and couldn't possibly interest several thousand people. Then my husband brought home George Schaller's *The Year of the Gorilla,* which proved to be one of the exciting highlights of my year's literary fare. Naturally, you say, gorillas *are* somewhat exciting — King Kong and all that. However, that's not the excitement I mean. While I was reading Schaller, I was completely engrossed in his gorillas and did not give my abandoned work a thought. But when I laid the book aside, I felt that curious seething sensation I get when something unexpectedly makes a communication strikingly relevant to my life and work. Here was a book about gorillas in which the author shot no gorillas and was attacked by no gorillas, was not even seriously menaced by gorillas and did not pretend to be filled constantly with alarming thoughts of being menaced by gorillas. It was a *quiet* book about gorillas, yet it was wholly absorbing. Did it interest me because I have a passion for gorillas? On the contrary, I have never cared overmuch for our fellow primates; my taste in the animal kingdom runs to otters and wolves. The secret of Schaller's book — and the instruction it communicated to me — was that loving and meticulous observation, recorded faithfully and without pomp or cant, can make almost anything absorbing. Heartened, I returned to my rough draft.

2. I had barely begun to read *The Ordeal of Change* by Eric Hoffer, when I encountered this, on page 2: "Faith, enthusiasm, and passionate intensity in general are substitutes for the self-confidence born of experience and the possession of skill. Where there is the necessary skill to move mountains there is no need for the faith that moves mountains." Hoffer was not writing about writers but about societies in transition; but suddenly my blood began to fizz as if it were carbonated, and I asked myself: Why,

then, do I sit around waiting for a fit of passionate intensity to carry me through the task of writing a novel, when I know, or ought to know, that after more than twenty years as a professional writer I have surely acquired enough skill to carry me through, even if I am *not* burning with faith through every paragraph?

The truth is that I have been afflicted with a misguided admiration for the fanatics of this world, the half-mad, bedeviled, possessed artists who take drugs, cut off their ears, shoot themselves or die raving. I say *misguided* not as a moral judgment but because these are hardly suitable subjects for emulation by the mother of over half a dozen children. Anyone who has ever tried it knows that it is impossible to be a responsible button-replacing, cooky-baking, dental-appointment-making housewife and a half-mad, possessed artist at the same time. And anyone who has written anything longer than a very short story knows that Hoffer is also right when he says, "Enthusiasm is ephemeral, and hence unserviceable for the long haul." For at some point in nearly every manuscript, enthusiasm dies or goes temporarily to sleep, and there is nothing left but hard, sometimes nauseating, work.

Surely I knew that already? But of course; still, there are a lot of things we "know" perfectly well but cannot accept or act upon until we meet them in a way that makes them cherished discoveries. It is possible that ideas wrested out of context or found in surprising surroundings may "take" better than those found where we are assiduously looking for them; it is also possible that the more desperately we search, the less likely we are to find anything at all. In one of my assiduous searches, I picked up *The Act of Creation* by Arthur Koestler, feeling certain that his exploration of the workings and sources of creativity would be one of the indispensables. All I retain after slogging through over seven hundred pages is the visual image of a monk in a saffron robe descending a holy mountain and meeting himself on the way up. I am not criticizing Mr. Koestler, but for me his was not the book to read at that time, in that mood. As for the up-and-down monk, read the book yourself and find out.

Listing the writers whose books have borne most directly and importantly on my work and my attitude toward it during the past year or two, I must include Charles Frankel, whose *Case for Modern Man* filled me with renewed conviction; C. S. Lewis, whose *Screwtape Letters* were, despite my abiding agnosticism, better than psychoanalysis; Thoreau, to whom I return again and again for sanity's sake; Norbert Wiener; Bertrand Russell; and the *Bhagavad-Gita.*

Let me make it clear: I am *not* recommending specific books. You may not care at all for Schaller, Hoffer, or even Thoreau, and they may give you nothing. Your problems are different and your answers will have to be different. You may even be a carefree, happy-go-lucky writer with no problems (that is, if there are unicorns in my garden and the moon is made of Gorgonzola). But if you are like me — and I have always assumed that my vices, fears, and disabilities are widely shared — you probably go through periods of intense effort or even panic, during which you may tend to become more narrowly selective in your reading, choosing either more and more how-to-write material, or, with equal desperation, one best seller after another. I simply want to suggest that you fight that tendency, widen your scope, and go farther afield; for the stimulus you need and the insight you may be waiting for may be waiting for you where you least expect it — in a quiet book about gorillas.

7

Letter to the World

BECAUSE I periodically change my reading habits out of a firm conviction that changing habits is A Good Thing, I haven't been reading *The New Yorker* for the past several years. I suppose I miss the cartoons most, but next to the cartoons I miss those little pieces at the bottom of the columns. I admit, however, that I have always felt a slight unease about a couple of these "departments." As a compulsive reader, I may have smiled at Letters We Never Finished Reading, but the only letters *I* never finish reading are from mortuaries; and as a compulsive writer, I have always shifted around nervously in my chair at the heading, Infatuation with the Sound of Own Words. I don't think I repeat myself so blatantly, but infatuated with the sound of my own words? Lordy, yes.

Mustn't I be, in order to be a writer? Aren't you?

Surely, unless he is just a cut-and-paste man putting together non-books, a writer must be infatuated with the run of his own thoughts, infatuated with the intricacies of his own fancies, infatuated with his own mind and its manifestation in words. He must be at once the focus and the source of what I call a necessary narcissism.

Because they express me most directly, I would rather — narcissistically — write journals, letters, and personal essays than write anything else you can name. (Oh, I would rather *have written* a great and magnificent novel, but I am talking about what I would rather *write,* which is another thing entirely and a distinction you might try drawing in your own case. It might shake you up a bit. It shakes *me,* at any rate.) Letter-writing is for me a vice and not a virtue. If you have written me a letter and I have not yet answered it, let me assure you that you cannot imagine what will power this non-answering takes. I force myself to pile mail up and answer it at intervals of several weeks, but my natural impulse is to answer everything five minutes after receipt. The dream of my life is to be permanently delegated by my publishers to turn out a never-ending Letter to the World, whether from the highlands of New Guinea, the cafés of Paris, or a one-star motel in Dullsville, N. Dak., I care not which, for "If I were confined to a corner of a garret all my days, like a spider," says Thoreau, "the world would be just as large to me while I had my thoughts about me." Oh to be allowed to be a true journalist, an actual lady (spider?) of letters, spinning them out day by day — such joy would be mine!

There is a large element of pure self-indulgence in this narcissistic infatuation, but I have found reputable support. Some time ago in a sociological anthology, I ran across an essay by C. Wright Mills, who agreed with me on the necessity (although Mills did not use my term) for a certain amount of narcissism. The other day my husband, who has as sharp an eye for what interests me as for what interests himself, brought home triumphantly a paperback volume by C. Wright Mills, *The Sociological Imagination,* which includes as an appendix this same remarkable essay, "On Intellectual Craftsmanship," from which I quote his advice to young sociologists, whom he urges to —

... set up a file, which is, I suppose, a sociologist's way of saying: keep a journal. . . . In this file, you, as an intellectual craftsman, will try to get together what you are doing intellectually and what you are experiencing as a person. . . . You will have often noticed how carefully accomplished thinkers treat their own minds, how closely they observe their development and organize their experience. The reason they treasure their smallest experiences is that, in the course of a lifetime, modern man has so very little personal experience and yet experience is so important as a source of original intellectual work. . . . By keeping an adequate file and thus developing self-reflective habits, you learn how to keep your inner world awake. . . . To maintain a file is to engage in the controlled experience.

Mills' essay is thirty-one pages long and well worth reading. If the word "file" bothers you, substitute "notebook" or "journal." Mills may have been addressing beginning sociologists, but the shoe fits anyone who works with his mind, and especially you and me.

So yes, I keep a journal — and I strongly urge that you do, too. Mine is not, unfortunately, always the journal I would like to keep, not the discursive, leisurely journal of my daydreams. Have you ever compared Somerset Maugham's *A Writer's Notebook* with Kenneth Roberts' *I Wanted to Write*? Maugham's selections from his notebooks give a portrait of the writer quietly, contemplatively working with his pen, unhurried, unharassed. Roberts' notes, on the other hand, are more often the wails and curses of a frustrated man, slaving under bad conditions and muttering and howling to himself. Both are worth reading — preferably together, I think.

My notebooks, although hardly publishable, are more Roberts than Maugham by far. Occasionally, a quiet reflection or a bit of description shows up, like the view from my window on a foggy day, "nothing visible beyond a spiky rim of telephone poles, TV antennae, leafless branches, all propping up a low gray sky like tent poles a sagging canvas" . . . but a more usual series of entries will read:

Finished rough draft. Needs cutting.
Toothache.
Try new ending. Patience, patience.
Royalties not here yet; what's holding them up?
Last two scripts in NY ten weeks and not a nibble.
No news from NY.
Ditto.
Still ditto.
At last, a sale. Only $125, but it's *something*.

This doesn't seem very self-reflective — but then I cheat a little by keeping carbons of some of my longer, lady-spider letters (my first book grew out of a year's collection), not a bad way to keep a journal at that. And yet, here and there, even in this most inadequate notebook are jottings of ideas, fragments of observation, one-sentence capsule plots or themes. Being a confirmed narcissist and a compulsive reader, I often sit down and read over a year or two, and sometimes an idea springs forth and takes me by the throat, perhaps an idea that has been slumbering there for half a decade. Not only that, but I recapture frames of mind, moments of insight, elation, and accomplishment, and I relive times of terrible depression and know by following their courses that they do, indeed, come to an end.

Infatuated with the sound of my own words? Of course I am. If what I'm thinking and saying doesn't fascinate *me*, what business have I to foist it upon *you*? It is part of the nature of a writer to be self-reflective, to be narcissistic, to gaze inward in absorbed concentration. The writer invites the world to listen to his unending soliloquy. Surely he must be listening, attentively, himself.

And taking notes.

8

A Good Word for Greed

THE other day I took note of the fact that my writing output seems to rise sharply after I buy myself a fistful of soft lead pencils or a 39¢ pack of onionskin. An aesthetic appreciation of tools and supplies, I concluded, might well be one of the primary predisposing factors in my career as a writer.

So it occurs to me today to take careful note of other events that are followed by a similar rise in work level, in energy, even, apparently, in imagination and inspiration. Are you with me? All right. I appear to enjoy a sudden spurt of work after (1) reading *The New York Times Book Review,* (2) reading *The Writer,* (3) reading a very good book, (4) reading a very bad book, (5) getting paid for something I've written, (6) sustaining a nasty financial setback, (7) rearranging my desk, and (8) going for a long automobile ride.

As for (1) and (2), they are too obvious to require comment. Reading about writing is always stimulating, stirring up all sorts of literary desires, ambitions, daydreams, plans, and ideas, and often giving me directly the advice or insight I've been needing. At first glance, (3) and (4) seem to cancel each other out, but I'm sure many of you react in the same fashion. The good books (or stories, or articles) show us the possibilities and fill us with the urge to achieve new levels of competence, while the bad ones bolster our egos

31

with the suspicion that we couldn't write such rotten stuff even if we tried. It's clear enough that (5) encourages me by reminding me that I am worth something, while (6) applies the sharp spur of necessity and at times the painful goad of desperation. I was going to say (7) is a housewifely energizer that can come out of the kitchen as well, culinary prowess rising briefly after the cupboards are cleaned and the copper bottoms of the pots and pans brought back to a shine with salt and vinegar, but I think it goes deeper than that. Fiddling with one's working environment must be an almost universal activity. If you can blame qualitative or quantitative deficiencies in your work on such things as bad lighting, poor acoustics, an uncomfortable chair, and a draft that keeps your feet frozen or your neck stiff, you needn't blame yourself. Naturally, each time you eliminate one of these scapegoat difficulties, you are forced to work a little harder until, happily, you light upon the next one. I myself can be found rearranging my desk — or moving everything to another part of the house — about once every two months, on the average.

Finally, (8). I put (8) down simply because I know it to be a fact, and I intended to dismiss it with a shrug of uncomprehension. However, after some long thought I have come to understand what is involved. I am a land-hungry person, and riding through the countryside raises my appetite for small valleys, windy crags, idyllic lake frontage, moist ravines, gravely beaches and even stretches of exposed and apparently barren desert. (I have discovered that when you get out of the car and use your feet, terrain that looks brown and barren at 70 mph suddenly becomes carpeted with wild flowers and alive with lizards and all sorts of fascinations, and I wouldn't mind owning a few acres of desert peach and Mormon tea and little scuttling horny toads, not at all.) So factor (8) is, primarily, a matter of greed.

We of the Great Psychiatric Society spend an astonishing amount of time analyzing people's motivations. We idolize nobility and purity of motive — selfless dedication in science and in the arts, for example — but when we encounter it, we tend not to believe it, and we dig tirelessly for the hidden crassness beneath the apparent altruism. Of course, almost nothing disturbs us more than having our own impulses misconstrued and being accused of "ulterior motives" — but I, for one, don't much like the opposite sort of thing either. For example, my irritation knew no bounds one year when I read on the front page of my income tax instructions a message beginning, "Every year more than 60 million individuals demonstrate their faith in America by filing income tax returns." I don't know why you file your income tax returns, but I do know why I file mine, and this involuntary enlistment in official hypocrisy made my gorge rise. I almost felt like cheating.

But to go on: Charity, for example, is always suspect. In the first place we know that the beneficence of giant corporations who give so magnificently for the public weal is not entirely without self-interest. And who among us, on this lower, penny-ante level, writes a check for the fight against muscular dystrophy or the fight to save the California redwoods without thinking, at least in passing, that his gift is, after all, tax-deductible? Some, perhaps, but not many.

Still, from the point of view of the scientist working on the problem of muscular dystrophy and the point of view of those who will enjoy each redwood saved from the devouring freeways, is charity's effect lessened appreciably by these considerations of motive? Likewise if an Olivier

mounts the stage out of sheer ego and an insatiable glut-
tony for applause, what care I as long as his Henry V
sends my spirits soaring and his crookbacked Richard
makes my blood congeal? With what does an actor wring
applause from his audience — with his motivation? or
with his ability?

You can turn to writing because Joe Scribbler made all
that money, and why shouldn't you? Or because there is
something poetic and fine in you, and you want to express
it . . . or because you hunger for glory . . . or because you
want to show your mother-in-law you're not the good-for-
nothing she seems to think you are . . . or because you are
possessed by an idea the world must hear . . . or because
you get a wild kick out of making something out of
nothing, a whole world out of thin air . . . or because a
talent with words seems to be the one asset you have, and
you have bills to pay. Any one of these, any combination
of them, or all of them at once can provide the driving
power to get you to your desk. How much does it matter
which?

No, I am not going to say that it does not matter at all.
Obviously some motivations will sustain you through
more severe trials than others, some will lessen your vul-
nerability to disappointment, some stiffen you against
compromises. But I cannot accept the notion that there is
a one-to-one relationship between a kind of nobility of
motivation and quality of result. (*His strength was as the
strength of ten because his heart was pure?*) It is not that
simple. We all have mixed motives, partly "noble" and
partly base, and partly unknown even to ourselves. Art
for art's sake alone, without thought of recompense, may
seem the purest motivation of all — if that is what purity
is (I am wondering what is impure about wanting to eat).
But pure motives alone never made great art, and dedica-

tion is no guarantee of genius. Without talent, pure and selfless dedication can result in trash and drivel, in simpering watercolors and limping verse, in wooden theatrics and off-key singing. On the other side of the coin, there are writers who claim to be writing for the money in it and nothing else, and yet, once engaged in their work, they are meticulous craftsmen or even consummate artists, making (in effort and time) great sacrifices in their drive to approach perfection.

I used to feel apologetic because I often sat down to write a story in order to pay a sheaf of bills, but no longer. I have discovered that some of my best work has been the happy result of financial pressure, and I am grateful to any motivation as long as it works. Regardless of what gets you to sit down at your desk and keeps you sitting there, it is skill and the pleasure of exercising your competence that makes your writing what it is. Almost any carrot will do, for once you roll the paper into the typewriter and begin to work, you hit the keys not because they'll pay the bills or bring you glory, but because *you're a writer*.

9

For Writing Out Loud!

O N those rare occasions when circumstances allow me
more than two consecutive hours of work at my desk,
I sometimes end up the victim of an attack of occupa-
tional laryngitis. I wouldn't expect much sympathy from
Maria Callas or Renata Tebaldi (after all, in my case a
slight laryngitis is hardly incapacitating), and even you,
though potentially sympathetic, may find it a little hard to
believe. Writer's cramp you could accept, or chipped nails
— but laryngitis?

Yes, laryngitis.

I've had trouble ever since our children reached fourth
grade and beyond, trying to convince them that I am of
no use when they need help with exercises in formal
grammar. I need only see them approaching with one of
those "language skills" books, and I know I'm in for it.

"I can't do it. I don't know how." *How come you're a
writer and you can't do it?* "I never learned." I peer at the
book. "I don't know a gerund from a bottle of Geritol."
That's not true; it can't be true. "It's true. Or almost. Only
a slight exaggeration." *Then how can you write?* "I write
by ear, that's how. I don't know the rules, and I don't
know how to diagram a sentence."

The child gives me a look heavy with suspicion. My
professed ignorance is a dodge, obviously. I just don't
want to be bothered.

Please, someone believe me. I am, I tell you honestly and sincerely, an ignoramus on the subject of English grammar. I learned to read before I went to school, and I read omnivorously and gluttonously. I swallowed the language whole, as it were, and wrote well enough by the time I was ten or so to be able to get through the balance of my school career unscathed and untouched by formal English instruction. I was always being excused from grammatical exercises so that I could be set to writing something instead. Teachers assumed that I knew the rules. After all, I never broke the more obvious ones. But I didn't know the rules. What I knew was the language. If I chose right from wrong, it was by sound — and by sound alone. I wrote entirely by ear.

And I still write by ear. Which is why I get a sore throat when I work hard.

No, I don't shout and declaim as I write; I don't even talk out loud, most of the time. I think perhaps if I could, if I had the luxury of privacy, I wouldn't get a sore throat or lose my voice. What I do indulge in is a constant mumbling, muttering, and whispering, subsiding (when anyone approaches) into a moving of the lips so frowned upon by the proponents of rapid reading; and I suspect that this repressed activity is what gives rise to muscle tension and precipitates laryngitis. Maybe if I could speak right out, I wouldn't have to be so knotted up.

However, even the risks of incurring a sore throat and of being suspected of a slight dottiness ("Who were you whispering to, Mama?" Um-m-m-m — nobody . . .) do not dissuade me. I shall not abandon my method. For I feel there is a special blight that afflicts writing which has managed, somehow or other, to reach paper without passing through the writer's vocal cords and what ought to be his critical ear. Music written by the congenitally tone-deaf, paintings done in the dead of night in a coal-pit and without so much as a candle — these would be comparable to writing engineered by those who have made marks on paper without listening with an intermediary ear.

Books for children are the most noticeable offenders, simply because they are the ones we are most likely to read aloud. The cheapest ones are usually the worst, but price is certainly no infallible guide. Janette Lowrey's *Poky Little Puppy* (A Little Golden Book) set me back twenty-six cents some years ago, but it reads beautifully, rollicking along, pell-mell, tumble-bumble, without a lapse. I've been reading it aloud, with pleasure, for almost twenty years. On the other hand, there are books selling for ten to fifteen times as much but written in a style which would refuse to be urged from its knees even by the voice of Richard Burton. There's no need to name any names; they are easy enough to find — terrible, tedious little volumes which you cannot read aloud.

Well, no, of course you *can*. But if you do, it is as if you were running a three-legged race with a stranger a foot shorter than yourself. You limp, you stagger, you fall flat on your face. The sentences all seem to be the wrong lengths. (This is, of course, not true. Only *some* of them are the wrong lengths.) You wonder if anybody but you has ever read the book aloud — and *you* never will again, not if you can help it. For these are the books you hate to see coming at you when you offer to read a bedtime story; these are the ones you gladly take along on automobile trips, hoping the children leave them under some motel bed; these are the ones you finally sneak to the school rummage sale, which is where your children probably got them in the first place.

So much for children's books. What about adult books? After all, you don't have to read adult books aloud — so my husband tells me, as he covers his ears. But the better books are the books you cannot resist reading aloud, the books that make you cry out, "Oh, listen to this!" And given your choice, wouldn't you rather write an oh-listen-to-this book than the kind of book which may yield up its content to visual skimming but fills your mouth with mush when you attempt to make it audible?

For writing is not something totally apart from speech. The best is even better when spoken, though the worst, instead of being improved, may betray itself badly when what we call "the dignity of print" is removed. The ear can catch awkward phrases, repetitions, boring rhythms, errors and confusions that can easily evade the eye. Ideally, I would work in a soundproof cell in which I could talk as loudly as I pleased; and once something was written, I would read it to a tape recorder and listen to it several times, with and without the script before me. Ideal conditions being unobtainable, I content myself with muttering as I compose and with moving my lips with every word of the finished composition. This bad habit of the semi-literate acts as a useful brake to keep the eager eye, half-blind with impatience, from racing uncritically to the end. (Speed-reading may be fine for busy executives faced with piles of long, boring reports, but I really doubt that writers should employ it *at all*.) So, moving my lips as I type, I put in my plea for writing out loud, and I urge you on (as the saying goes) with hoarse cries.

10

The Writer as Hero

IF I wanted to dig into the mouldering correspondence — which at last bulked larger than the ill-fated novel it was *anent* — I could find the exact quote for you, but I hesitate to poke into that old literary wound of mine. Briefly, however: I had a rousing opening chapter and a synopsis of this novel, a comic novel about a writer. I won't go into the details of how the project fell apart and the novel wound up, like about six others I have, stowed away in a cardboard box, except that it was a classic case of too many cooks spoiling my broth of a book until the taste of it turned my stomach. I was, in a word, *over-advised*.

The major piece of advice I was given was that I should not write a novel about a writer. Writers do not make good heroes. Readers do not want to read about writers. Novels about writers do not sell.

There was a lot of other advice, ranging from censoring out illegitimate children to discovering uranium on my hero's property, until at last I was put on a regime of tranquilizers and the book was consigned to the box where it has lain ever since. It was my fault, of course. I should have shut my ears, stopped opening all mail from New York, and written what I started out to write. But I was younger and greener then and didn't have the sense to see what was happening until it was too late.

40

Years later, still haunted by the question: Why *not* a writer as a hero?, I decided to consult with and observe the following writer-heroes: Manley Halliday (of *The Disenchanted,* by Budd Schulberg), Sam Silver (*The Sound of Bow Bells,* Jerome Weidman), Youngblood Hawke (*Youngblood Hawke,* Herman Wouk), Alec Barr (*The Honey Badger,* Robert Ruark), Brendan Tierney (*An Answer from Limbo,* Brian Moore), F. Hilary Stevens (*Mrs. Stevens Hears the Mermaids Singing,* May Sarton), and Bertram Flax (*The Hack,* Wilfrid Sheed). There are a number of others I could have included, but I felt that too many would make for an unwieldy session, so I limited myself to these seven.

(Obvious preliminary statement: it cannot be true that novels about writers don't sell. If these novels hadn't sold to some extent, I'd never have been able to find them in the public library or at the bookstore.)

The first thing I discovered about writer-heroes is that they don't write. Or at least they hardly ever write. By that I mean that they don't write *in the reader's presence.* The only one of the seven whose writing we actually see is Bertram Flax, the Catholic hack whose work appears in *The Tiny Messenger,* and *The Companions of St. Agatha.* Wilfrid Sheed quotes liberally from the writings of Bert Flax, but everybody else's work has to be taken almost entirely on faith or on second-hand description and fragments of synopsis. Oh, they put in the hours at writing (or so we are told) — for example, we see Youngblood Hawke repairing to his labors and we clock how long he stays there, and now and then we are thrown a few scraps of plot from one of his novels. But while Manley Halliday and Shep Stearns fake out a scenario for a movie I'm glad I never had to see, and while we are aware that Sam Silver is turning pieces of his own life into marketable fiction, we have in most cases nothing much to go on. I am not saying that we don't believe these writers are writing. I am positive Brendan Tierney writes — nothing else could possibly explain what he does to (or fails to do for) his wife Jane and his mother Eileen. But exactly *what* he is writing, I couldn't say.

Why don't writer-heroes write? Paul Gallico says in *Confessions of a Story Writer,* "Nothing is quite so static and unromantic as a gent parked on his hams punching a typewriter . . ." And this was underlined by my adviser, who insisted that after all I couldn't write a whole novel in which my hero did nothing but sit and think! It would appear, then, that a writer writing is boring, whereas a writer *not* writing, a writer in the grip of a writer's block, swilling alcohol, hitting his wife, running around with other women, neglecting his kids, getting embroiled in tax troubles, having hallucinations and dying — that's different.

All right. Ruefully we admit it may be boring, though why that should stop us I don't know; other writers have been boring me for years with long descriptions of bull fighting, big-game hunting, tax troubles. . . . However, there's another reason why most writer-heroes don't write. Hear Vladimir Nabokov in *Bend Sinister:* ". . . the author and his yes-characters assert that the hero is a 'great artist' or a 'great poet' without, however, bringing any proofs (reproductions of his paintings, samples of his poetry), indeed, taking care *not* to bring any such proofs since any samples would be sure to fall short of the reader's expectations and fancy." No wonder only Bert Flax, the hack, is seen writing. A writer who is himself a few cuts below absolute greatness is going to have a hard time depicting a hero who is a great writer. Believe me, if I were capable of dreaming up the plot of a masterpiece or the first

twenty lines of a deathless poem, I'd think twice before
I'd invent some fictitious writer by the name of Aloysius
Bleistift and credit *him* with them!

What can a writer do but assemble his yes-characters
and then try to make his writer-hero behave in writer-
fashion? — that is, in a manner we have known or believed one or another writer to have behaved in. We end
up believing that Youngblood Hawke is a great writer because of Thomas Wolfe, believing Manley Halliday a
tragic, ruined talent because of F. Scott Fitzgerald, and
deciding that Alec Barr somehow finds time to write because Robert Ruark found time to write, didn't he? No,
there's nothing reprehensible about this. Writers have to
do it all the time. Write about a great cook and there's
no way I know of to get the taste across on paper; write
about a great violinist and short of putting a long-play
record in a pocket on the back cover, what can you do?
We don't demand samples of anything else, why of
writing?

However, I happened to be reading *The Horse's Mouth*
by Joyce Cary in between bouts of reading about Sam and
Alec and Youngblood and the rest, and I cannot help
making a comparison. Cary made me believe more deeply
in Gulley Jimson as an artist than most of the other
writers were able to make me believe in their heroes as
writers, despite the fact that no paintings were repro-
duced in the text and there weren't many yes-characters
of a convincing authority. I couldn't see any of Jimson's
paintings, but what I *did* see was all the world with Jimson's eye. I saw the phantasms of colors and shapes that
rose up before him, the dream-paintings that flew through
his head, and if what I experienced wasn't the eye-and-
mind of an artist, it was surely the most gloriously complete counterfeit imaginable. I believed in Gulley Jimson

because of the way he saw the world — and I am still waiting to meet a Gulley Jimson who writes.

Writing aside, how are these writer-heroes simply as heroes? Well, I know we don't expect truly heroic heroes in fiction any more — admirable heroes are left to those who write glory-ographies in election years. But the one emotional response that kept recurring in me as I read was pity. I didn't pity all of them, but I certainly pitied most of them — a sorry lot, swindled and used and victimized by women and publishers and agents and friends, hopeless with money and worse without it, making their families miserable and not exactly rolling in joy themselves. (Incidentally, tell me, why did I never pity Gulley Jimson? He was magnificently heroic, ruthless, unscrupulous, demented, and never, not even in direct adversity, *never* pitiable.) Are we writers, I kept thinking, really such dismal people?

It's funny. I didn't mean to take that old advice to heart, but I checked over my files the other day and can report that only one out of about 140 short stories I've written has a writer as a protagonist, and that was only a device by which to get the story rooted out and told. I haven't written anything with a writer as hero — except, to be sure, when writing about Heroic Me. So I have never tested myself against this challenge, and unless I some day get the courage to attack that old comic novel again, I probably never will. I don't suppose my writer-hero was going to be especially heroic or admirable either, come to think of it, and although I had included some samples of his work, I had taken pains to make him a popular novelist of uncertain and fluctuating talent, so that I didn't have to prove him a great writer at all.

I don't wish to leave the impression that the seven books I've mentioned are not worth reading. They are all, in various ways, well worth the time of any writer-reader. The Brian Moore novel is unforgettable; you will recognize bits of yourself in each of the six heroes and one heroine, and you will find their lives edifying and chastening at the very least.

But I find I have to keep up my spirits when contemplating the Writer as Hero by remembering my all-time favorite writer-heroine, Charlotte A. Cavatica (*Charlotte's Web,* E. B. White), whose works her creator presents *in toto* and of whom it is said at the end, "She was in a class by herself. It is not often that someone comes along who is a true friend and a good writer. Charlotte was both."

11

A Leg Up for Ditched Centipedes

YOU know that centipede, I'm sure, who lay distracted in the ditch because he didn't know which leg came after which — a sad case, but not altogether hopeless.

It happened that most of the family were lounging around the living room when the mail arrived this noon. I began reading this particular letter to myself, but after I choked on a weird little noise halfway between a snicker and a sob, I found everybody looking at me and I had to start over again, this time aloud.

My correspondent had been reading an article on how and where to unearth ideas, and she was, she said, amazed that serious writers should need such direction. "My files are overflowing," she wrote, "with notes and suggestions, and on my desk at the moment are manuscripts in all stages of completion: two book reviews, an article for a magazine, a novelette, a short story, a juvenile, and background material for a murder mystery."

I giggled (nervously) and read on: "Now, before you can say, 'Doesn't *she* sound smug,' let me assure you that this is a problem with a capital P. I've got so much to write that *nothing* gets written! I'm so confused with ideas that I don't even know where to start. I just sit at the desk trying to decide which is more important, then finally say to myself, 'I'll be able to think better tomorrow. Tonight, I'll just go to bed and read instead.'"

Someone snorted, possibly my husband. I wasn't looking anyone in the eye at that moment, but rather hiding behind the letter to the best of my ability. I went on reading anyway, from "Would you be kind enough to tell me how you deal with this problem?" to the final, unbearable sentence, "What time there is is too precious to waste just sitting staring into space!"

General laughter, mine somewhat hollow.

So I'm sitting here at my desk, on which there are a notebook of ideas and half-done essays, two rough drafts of juvenile books, one long short story in the process of being cut in half, a second draft of a new story, a thick folder of incomplete drafts and synopses, a master list of eighty-three short-story ideas culled from my journals, notes for a non-fiction book, and the outline for an essay series. That's *this* desk. Unfinished novels are around and about another desk. And then there's the filing cabinet . . .

Still, there is something to be said in favor of asking my advice on this problem. In some ways, only the blind *can* lead the blind. Only the blind can really understand; only the blind who have triumphed over blindness can show others the way.

I claim no major triumph, but I have managed occasional small victories. Certainly I *understand,* for indecision over what I ought to be working on is one of the worst stumbling blocks I have ever encountered. (Notice that word "ought" — we'll get back to it later.) I'm not sure that anyone not so afflicted can possibly realize how miserable this embarrassment of riches can be. Furthermore, it is frighteningly cumulative: You start with a little hesitation in front of two or three tempting ideas, and then while you stand there more and more of them arrive, until your stumbling block is a veritable wall at the foot of which you are rooted in a wordless paralysis.

"Do you divide your day into blocks of time," my correspondent asks, "and devote so much to each article and story you're working on, or do you permit yourself to do only one at a time? What happens when you're working on your monthly column and you suddenly get a strong and exciting idea for a new short story? How do you sandwich in those books you write as well?"

I don't have enough day to divide into blocks of time, except that I always regard my evenings as free from scheduled work — free to be spent on reading and study, or, if I am fortunate, on some strong and exciting idea. (Strong and exciting ideas are the only ones that can survive the noisy and populated evenings in this house, anyway.) As it is, I divide the *month* into blocks of time, setting deadlines for completing an essay, a draft of a story, a cutting-and-revision, or whatever — but, I assure you, all is subject to change without notice. No schedule should ever be so rigid as to allow no time for that sudden inspiration; strong and exciting ideas should be attended to when they come, even if a day or a week be thrown out of joint.

A second practical move which allows me to forget (for a while) the other clamoring possibilities ("Maybe you ought to be working on *me* . . . maybe you could finish *me* faster . . . maybe some editor would buy *me* . . .") is to schedule a cooling-off period for every draft of every script. Knowing that a time is approaching when I can give one of those ideas my attention, I can for the time being sweep the desk and my mind clear of everything but the script at hand.

However, I still find it difficult to get down to work on something that I know is going to take months and months, even though I promise myself small holidays for smaller scripts. It is so much easier to write a continuous flood of stories, essays, and personal letters. Small victories are cheap and also alluring. The more I think of it, the more I am convinced that the real question to be faced by people like me is *not*, "What ought I to be working on?" or, as my correspondent put it, "Which is more important?" For the very way I put the question implies that there is one inescapably right answer — and *is* there, really? And even if there is, how on earth could anyone possibly be certain of it beforehand? Why should I, for example, assume that the longest and hardest thing is the thing I ought to be doing right now?

I suggest that you tell yourself there *is* no one thing you ought to be writing. The only sure thing is that you ought to be writing instead of dithering. So if need be, just chant an eenie-meenie choosing rhyme and stab with your forefinger — and then get everything else *off your desk*.

I know that what we all want is to be seized by a fiery conviction that one particular thing is the right thing for us to be doing at this particular time. But for people of many ideas such moments of absolute certainty rarely arrive; you must simply be resigned to this. It's not such a bad condition to be resigned to at that. At least when one idea sours, all is not lost. Abandon it for the time being and stab again. Eenie-meenie! — Sooner or later something takes hold and runs its course to a triumphant conclusion.

Console yourselves: Think of Leonardo da Vinci, a man of many ideas, many talents. Too many ideas, too many talents? Well, my encyclopedia says, "Indeed, he had so many skills that he had little time to bring any one to completion." Poor Leonardo! Surely there were days when he hardly knew what to do first, and I can easily imagine that in final desperation he often chanted the 15th-century Italian equivalent of eenie-meenie-miney-mo — and just grabbed.

Fellow centipedes, *any* leg first will get you out of the ditch, and once you start moving, you will get around to using all your legs in due time. *No choice you make can possibly be as bad as making no choice at all.*

12

Great Aspirations and Dreadful Despairs

WHO can resist a new year? Even those who declare themselves firmly resolved against resolutions will nevertheless be caught taking a deeper breath on or about January first. The mood is as infectious as the common cold; we breathe in the virus of new beginnings, and we sneeze out, "I resolve . . ."

I could write a fine list of resolutions for you (I am a top-notch thinker-upper of improvements for other people), but I'm not going to do it. No, rather than tell you what resolutions to make, I am going to tell you how to make whatever resolutions you want to make *so that you can keep them.*

Those who were completely satisfied with last year should read no further; this is not for you. Nor is it for you who believe that whatever was wrong with last year was due to a kink in your horoscope or can be blamed on your children, your wife, the wrong wattage in your desk lamp, the wrong typeface in your portable, or a bevy of recent Sarah Lawrence graduates stationed in each of the editorial offices in New York, whose duty it is to intercept manuscripts from you and send them back unread. If you are of that persuasion, nothing you resolve to do can help. Give up writing. Go back to the kitchen and learn to make Greek pastry. Wash all the woodwork every week. Resolve to spend next year perfecting your golf game or

getting elected chairman of the grievance committee
down at the plant.

Now. Those of you who are still with me please understand that I am an authority on the subject of resolutions,
agenda, and all manner of lists. The first chapter of my
first book is something of a manual on list-management,
and in fact the entire book revolves more or less on the
theme of resolutions and the futility thereof. I mention
this mainly to indicate that I have given a great deal of
thought over a considerable length of time to the matter
of resolutions and also to the matter of the kind of people
who habitually make resolutions — and break them.

After a long study of this kind of person (my laboratory
subject being myself), I have concluded that the main
reason so many resolutions are made only to be broken
is that resolution-makers are always people given to great
aspirations and subject to dreadful despairs. They in-
variably set impossible goals for themselves, and then approach the attainment of these goals with an all-or-nothing
frame of mind. "I resolve to lose X pounds every week,
without fail," they say, or, "I resolve to write X words
every day, do or die." And since an all-or-nothing frame
of mind means that one is unwilling to settle for anything
in between, it is easy to predict what happens. The first
week in which no pound is lost, why, *all* is lost, and our fat
would-be dieter goes off to drown her sorrows in a choco-
late malted. Likewise, the first day in which X words do
not get written, all is lost in that cause too; the would-be
writer decides wordlessly that he can never make it, and
he stops trying.

There is a way — and it may be the only way — to fight
this problem, and that is to frame your resolutions so that
they set no standards by which you must judge your performance, pass or fail, every day or every week. For if you

set no inflexible mark at which you reckon success, you will have no place at which to consign yourself to failure, and you can work along steadily in a happy middle ground of striving. Which is, some think, the best place to be most of your life anyway.

For examples, I give you *my* resolutions:

1. On the assumption that I am going to be reading anyway, I shall devote some part of my reading to the best in literature — to classics and acknowledged modern masterpieces. (I think I may even be brave and start with *Orlando* and *Mrs. Dalloway,* for, in case you have been wondering, *I* am the one who has been, all these years, afraid of Virginia Woolf.)

2. On the assumption that I do not already know everything worth knowing, I am also going to invest part of my reading time in some topic of study relatively new to me. (I have already chosen my subject, ecology.)

3. Because there is always less time in the day than I need, I shall try to get rid of some of my time-wasting habits and form better ones to replace them. (I could, for example, stop checking for mail every half hour — especially since for me that means leaving the house and walking to the RFD box!)

4. Because I feel that nobody should go on indefinitely either attempting to repeat old successes or grubbing away in the barren ground of old failures, I shall begin exploring some field of writing new to me, shall study it, and shall give myself a fair trial within its borders. (This is not exactly cricket, for I chose my new field of endeavor some time ago, and have already begun; still, I resolve to continue. My choice: children's books.)

5. Finally, I resolve to set a primary goal for the year and to bend the major part of my energy and time toward

its accomplishment. (My goal: another book on its way to print.)

Please note that the foregoing resolutions do not set any marks of absolute success; to fall short of them does not mean absolute failure. I did not make a long list of books to read, without fail; and I did not say I intended to *master* Hindustani in twelve months' time, but only that I intended to *study* ecology. Each resolution contains words such as *some, part, begin, try,* etc. Even the phrase *on its way to print* allows for a comfortable latitude in interpretation. With resolutions of that sort, an inferior day's work is not failure but only just a little less successful, and I can hope to do better the next day.

My resolutions may not appeal to you at all. But whatever you do resolve — to try confessions, to read Shakespeare, to resign from the bridge club, to study astronomy — do *not* resolve to write 2,000 words a day, do or die; for if you are the kind of person I am, you will find that the first time you don't write those 2,000 words the whole project will die, right on the spot.

There is nothing wrong with high goals and great aspirations, but if you are given to dreadful despairs as well, take pains not to set marks that make your performance constantly measurable, day by day. For our kind of person (and I don't think any other kind ever *makes* resolutions) the best and only course is to resolve

NOT to be perfect, but to improve;

NOT to succeed, but to try;

NOT to achieve, but to keep on working.

13

In Praise of a Café-au-Lait Bat

I HAVE not yet gotten around to making a list of Books Every Writer Should Own. Every time I think of embarking upon the project, I remember that the most famous writer I ever knew (well, the *only* famous writer I ever knew) was at the time I knew him the humble owner of but two pairs of trousers. He was in those days employed at sweeping out the back room of a grocery store, and although I recall that he carried with him at one time or another a copy of T. S. Eliot's *Four Quartets*, it may have been a library book. I now own almost all of his books, and he, I suppose, could buy the entire contents of my library without turning a financial hair; but when I knew him, over twenty years ago, he may not have owned any books at all.

Still, these are more affluent days for almost all of us, and most writers own at least a few books. If I were to proceed with the aforementioned list, I would begin with a good dictionary, add a copy of Roget's *Thesaurus* and then either Fowler's *Modern English Usage* or Margaret Nicholson's *Dictionary of Modern American Usage*. Beyond that, much depends on what kind of writer you are. I like to have a good encyclopedia handy, plus a reasonably up-to-date atlas and a current *World Almanac*. Rich writers should of course own a tax guide; the rest of us, however, might do better with a copy of *A Cookbook for Poor Poets and Others,* by Ann Rogers, which (unless you are already pretending to the butcher that you own a dog) will pay for itself within a month. I see also on my desk a dictionary of quotations, nice to browse in, and a copy of a little book by Sir Ernest Gowers, called *Plain Words.* Sir Ernest's work is useful even when I don't open it; a glance at the title alone serves as a bracing rebuke.

Only a dictionary is indispensable. Yet, if I had to choose but one book, you could not part me from a shabby volume entitled *The Working Principles of Rhetoric,* by John Franklin Genung (Ginn and Company, 1900), which I used to dip into when I was a very young girl. If any book really shoved me into the path that led to my being a writer, this was it. It was in Genung that I first met that classic, galloping example of onomatopoeia from Virgil, *"Quadrupedante putrem sonitu quatit ungula campum"* (Heigh-ho, Silver — *away!*), which I found, at the age of ten or so, fearfully exciting stuff. I couldn't really translate it then, and I can't now, but the sound of hoofbeats was enough to stir me. Imagine being able to make language behave so marvelously! At that moment, I think, I was off and running.

Still, you can get along without old Genung (it was old Genung even then) and probably without anything beyond a thirty-nine-cent tablet and a sharp pencil. But getting excited about books is a vice of mine — I have *no* moderation in the matter — and being given the chance to do it in print is beyond resisting, especially when I run across a book like the one I have sitting by the side of the typewriter right now. It is only forty-three pages long and a number of the pages are pictures, so I'm not asking too much when I implore you to beg, borrow, steal, or even buy a copy of *The Bat-Poet,* by Randall Jarrell. It is not a brand-new book (it came out in 1964) but you may well have missed it, as I did at first, despite the fact that it is all about writing. You will find it in the children's book section of the bookstore or public library, and if you are shy about getting it for yourself, you can pretend you're getting it for a favorite niece. If you do buy it, you might even give it away to a favorite niece after you've read it, provided there's a niece you like *that* well.

However, to enjoy *The Bat-Poet* one need not have a child in mind or even have a taste for children's books. It is sufficient merely to be a writer, or a would-be writer, or even just a reader — but best of all, a writer.

I have, since old Genung, read a lot of books about writing. I have nowhere else read such a deep and crystal-clear story of what it means and how it feels to be a writer — and also, of course, what it means and how it feels to be a bat. It is all there, though you may not even realize the first time through what you have read. But it *is* all there — all about poets and poems and readers of poems, all about a writer's hopes and disappointments and triumphs. If you can read the chipmunk's reactions to the bat-poet's poems without your heart leaping for joy, then your motives for writing must be far different from mine. And then there's the affair of the cardinal, the ideal subject who simply refused to be written about. How many cardinals have I encountered in my life as a writer, have watched, have thought about, have marveled at, have even taken notes on, and then have abandoned in despair, never knowing exactly why I could not put them into words! " 'That's *queer,*' the chipmunk said." — But not uncommon, say I, ruefully.

Earlier in this book, talking about books with writer-heroes, I noted how few fictitious writers ever write anything that we are allowed to read. But Randall Jarrell's bat-poet's poems are quoted; and because the late Mr.

Jarrell was an excellent poet, this bat is an excellent poet, too. I don't think I shall ever see a bat again without remembering, "A bat is born, Naked and blind and pale..." But I mustn't begin to quote, for I wouldn't know where to stop, and, as I said, the book is only 43 pages long and has a lot of pictures, which, incidentally, were done by the incomparable Maurice Sendak, who also illustrated Mr. Jarrell's lovely fable, *The Animal Family*.

I don't consult old Genung any more for rhetorical aid. I keep it for what it means to me. Some day, I think, when some very young poets have grown to maturity, there will be battered copies of *The Bat-Poet* cherished on *their* shelves for the same reason; and I wish for them and for their poems an audience made up of a high percentage of chipmunks. They will know what I mean.

14

Peaks and Valleys, but No Plateaus

A FEW years ago, *The Reader's Digest* reprinted something of mine. I don't remember now what it was, but I do remember that someone said to me at the time, "Well, now you must feel you've really *arrived!*"

I had been writing for well over a decade, had one book published and another on the way, had appeared in numbers of magazines, had written for both radio and television, and couldn't help finding it difficult to regard being *Digested* as the criterion of "arrival." How curious, I thought; people's ideas of literary arrival are certainly different. I didn't stop, however, to ask myself what *I* would consider the criterion of arrival. If I had, I might have been satisfied, I readily admit, with some pat answer like "best seller" or "movie rights" or "Pulitzer Prize," depending of course on how hard I wanted to make it for myself to qualify.

If I had given it more thought, however, I might have wound up in deep perplexity. Has a writer arrived when he receives a dollar a word from a magazine of several hundred thousand circulation, national distribution, and no literary standing? Or, on the other hand, has he arrived when he receives his two free contributor's copies (and no money) from a journal of small circulation, limited distribution, and considerable critical repute? Has a writer arrived when he has a book published? A play televised?

A short piece anthologized? Has a writer arrived when he begins to get a steady supply of fan mail? Is appearance in *The New Yorker* the sure sign of arrival? How about translation into half a dozen languages?

If these are acceptable criteria for arrival, then except for my failure to have achieved the pages of *The New Yorker*, I have arrived any number of times. But it seems to me that shortly after I arrive, I always leave; and I have begun to feel strongly that I have no penultimate destination whatsoever, only the final one we all share.

I have never felt "arrived" — not as I imagine this state of content and satisfaction to be, in the minds of its contemplators, that is. One of my cherished ambitions for many years was to become a columnist. Well, I am one. I have arrived! Of course, I can enter a minor quibble at this point; what I really want is a column in which I can talk about anything at all, not just anything to do with the art and business of communication through words. I'd like carte blanche to write about cooking, politics, fashion, philosophy, children, history, whatever comes forth when I reach into my mind — and you who have read my books know what a ragbag mentality *I* have. Still, although I have limitations set upon me, they are not unbearably stringent. I *am* a columnist, I do write a column; unquestionably, I have arrived.

Well, it's true: whenever I get a column written and am satisfied with it, I have arrived. But I never unpack and settle down.

For the landscape as I see it does not consist of a single eminence I am attempting to scale, nor is it dominated by some great, high plateau upon which dwell the writers who have arrived, a plateau to whose rarefied level we all aspire. No, the literary terrain through which we travel is a jumble of peaks and valleys — *and no plateaus.* When any of us reaches a summit, he sits down, has his lunch, inscribes his name in the register — and then puts on his knapsack again and descends. Nobody sets up housekeeping at the top. As for the next peak, well, the skill you gain and the strength you build on one, you can certainly use on the next, but you never climb one mountain starting from the top of another. Each time, alas, you begin from the bottom — and, leaving the metaphor aside, *with blank paper.*

I am pretty sure that even those writers the man in the street considers long since arrived feel exactly this way. These sentences of John Steinbeck's bear repeating: "When I face the desolate impossibility of writing five hundred pages, a sick sense of failure falls on me and I know I can never do it. This happens every time."

This happens every time. Each new undertaking is a fresh and often a painful challenge. And because, like many mountain climbers, the writer chooses ever higher and more difficult climbs to attempt, arrival may indeed grow progressively harder instead of easier. Readers in their innocence may think a writer has "arrived," for they see him only when he pauses at one summit after another; during the long and arduous ascents, he is out of sight. To them, at their distance, a succession of peaks blurs into that high and untaxing plateau across which the writer appears to be strolling easily — but *he* knows how many times he has been down and up, down and up, down again, and with exasperating effort, up. Public acclaim and even the money may last from peak to peak, but they don't do the writer's work for him.

Arrival is exhilarating but very temporary. And perhaps you arrive as surely with that first acceptance from some obscure magazine as you may years later with a twenty-three-week stand on the best seller list. All I know is that I have arrived and departed as often as a commuter train. My knapsack is nearly always on my back, and I hope I die with my climbing boots on, my ice ax in my hand.

15

Writers as Rememberers

THE poet Shelley wanted to reform the world. As anyone can tell, he didn't. But much as I consider the world in dire need of changing, I shall not mourn this unachieved ambition. Reforms come and go, often leaving little trace, and mad Shelley's mind may have been better fit for writing odes than for drawing up social blueprints.

In 1817 Shelley wrote "Ozymandias," and now, a century and a half later, I recite it to myself and shiver, seeing in my mind's eye those "trunkless legs of stone," that arrogant head fallen to the sand:

> "My name is Ozymandias, King of Kings;
> Look on my works, ye Mighty, and despair!"
> Nothing beside remains. Round the decay
> Of that colossal wreck, boundless and bare
> The lone and level sands stretch far away.

Made thoughtful, I remember the Colossus of Rhodes, the Hanging Gardens of Babylon, the Pyramids of Egypt . . .

Once there were more than eighty pyramids biting into the blazing Egyptian sky. Most of them are rubble now; and can you name, without consulting a book, the builders of the greatest three that remain? Khufu, Khafre, Menkaure; I knew only the first, and by a Greek name at that, and I had to look up the other two in the encyclopedia.

When an Egyptian king acceded to the throne, he began at once the preparations for his tomb. Most of us are not so much interested in the glories of our future interment, but we are all, nevertheless, would-be pyramid-builders. Each of us, admit it or not, would be pleased to have a pyramid of one sort or another to leave behind.

Man desires immortality, but, being man, he tends to desire it not in that vast and terrifying eternity he cannot really imagine, but — more cozily — among his fellow men. He is rather less concerned with his immortal soul than with the relative immortality of his very mortal and transient ego. What he hankers after is a small, comprehensible, earthly immortality: to be remembered here, after he is gone.

You and I who write attempt to build our pyramids out of words. But in our writing, we are not only seekers after immortality but also its custodians; sometimes, even, its bestowers. For what is chosen to be remembered is in large part chosen by us. We are foremost among the rememberers; like ancient grandfathers reciting illustrious genealogies, we do the remembering for our tribe.

I am not being arrogant. This is the truth. Unsung heroes are not heroes beyond their mortal spans. If there were no poets, no storytellers, no chroniclers, no writers, heroes would remain unsung and deeds unremembered, all doomed to the obliteration of silence. Only in the telling can deeds and dreams, doers and dreamers, be kept alive, be made immortal — that is to say, *remembered.*

But (you say) I am only me. I write nothing earthshaking, no tales of valor or of iniquity, no accounts of the doings of heroes. I write only stories, only trivial verses, only fabrications and imaginings, only small events from the small corner of my own world. What have I to do with immortality?

True enough, you *are* only you. But turn it around: Only *you* are you; no one else is you. There are thoughts only you have. There are things only you can say. There are events to which only you can play chronicler. And if you do not deal in reality, why, dreams are a reality, too. Fiction *is* real. What men in their reveries spin out of cobwebs and moonbeams, giving "to airy nothing a local habitation and a name" — these are as pertinent to an understanding of humanity as the specifications of any pyramid. As for trivia, Samuel Pepys recorded a lot of trivia in his diary, but, faced with the necessity of a choice, I would sacrifice a whole pyramid to know the similar secrets of the heart and mind of just one ordinary Egyptian who was there when the stones were placed. Tear it down, level it, and give me a Samuel Pepys of 2500 B.C. instead. (And you might note in passing that if the immortal Pepys had not kept that diary, his would be only another name on a list of secretaries of the Admiralty, with a footnote on shipbuilding — and you and I would never have heard of him.)

So only you are you. If you value this uniqueness of yours, you will be yourself, speak out as yourself, and bring to every writing task as much of yourself as you can muster. Is this concern with self and its expression an ignoble egotism, selfish and petty? On the contrary, one of the greatest riches of mankind is this myriad variation, selves like snowflakes, no two alike. When each of us chooses different things to record, to remember, to nominate for immortality, we insure the memory of as wide and detailed a view of man as possible, and this enriches us all, now and in the future.

Last year, however, something like twenty-eight thousand books, over seventeen hundred daily papers, and eight thousand magazines and journals were published in the

United States. How much of all this wordage will survive? Will any of mine? Will any of yours? And for how long? This, like the crumbling of pyramids, is a sobering thought. But man has always been possessed of a certain mad optimism which keeps him at this pyramid-building business of his, and we writers are no less afflicted than the general run of the population, including pharaohs.

But did you know that Shelley spent his first honeymoon distributing copies of an inflammatory pamphlet, some of which he rolled up, thrust into bottles, and set adrift? There's optimism for you; or madness, if you wish. And yet, isn't that what we're all doing, more or less? Immortality: that's when one of your bottles washes up on the beach and somebody finds it. (Or when, dear Shelley, people are still reading "Ozymandias" one hundred and fifty years after you put it on paper.)

Funny thing, though. Pyramids crumble, bottles come uncorked and sink without a trace, and not having written an "Ozymandias," I have small chance of being read even a quarter of a century from now. And that is, frankly, the story of much of man's endeavor on this parlous planet. Yet for some reason I keep caring very much about what I put into those bottles of mine.

One piece of good sense, said Thoreau (who had no use at all for pyramids), *would be more memorable than a monument as high as the moon.*

16

One, Two, Three . . .

A CASUAL thumbing of my notebook and a quick prowl through the clutter on my desk would suffice to uphold my claim, as follows: I am one of the world's great planners.

In my notebook, plans spring forth every few pages — outlines of this, schedules for that, agenda headed SPRING, other agenda under more explicit headings ("Week of Apr. 10–16"), and so on. On my desk — along with the library books, the jar of congealed rubber cement with its lid askew, the frozen orange juice can (full of defunct ball-point pens, broken pencils, and a ghastly black-stained toothbrush belonging to my typewriter), and the doll's teapot which holds a bouquet of three dead dandelions and a clover blossom — you will find another agenda on a sheet of green paper, and to the right of the typewriter, a yellow page with the outline from which I trust this discourse will emerge.

Butterflies do come out of cocoons, so I bend my attention optimistically upon this tangle of scribbling. Besides, in the middle of the page I see numbers (1) and (2), therefore, obviously, the work in hand has been planned with some care; there is nothing in which we Americans put more faith than enumerations. The weakest and draftiest argument in the world sounds fine when you lay it out with numbers (1), (2), (3). I am probably as addicted a victim-practitioner of this fallacy as you may find. My agenda and outlines are always neatly numbered. Well, numbered, anyway.

Until a few minutes ago I was in the middle of a fourteen-chapter juvenile, outlined carefully, so many pages to be written per chapter, so many days to be devoted to the task, etc., etc., etc. I have stopped to write this little piece on planning because it occurred to me that you could no doubt use my seasoned advice on the topic. It also occurred to me that I cannot face Chapter Nine even though the date for its completion is staring me in the face and will soon, if I turn my calendar pages on time, be flipped out of sight. And one of the major reasons I cannot face Chapter Nine is that Chapter Eight somehow failed to cover the enumerated topics listed under (8) on my outline, and there appears to be insufficient preparation for the material approaching in Chapter Nine.

But that's enough about *that* outline. A closer look at *this* outline shows me that the two numbers (1) and (2) are followed by two words, *work* and *time*. That seems to be almost all that's clearly legible on this side of the page, but it will do. It's enough to get me on with the task.

Planning, to be concise, has two aspects: work and time. You plan work by breaking it down into sections and subsections, tasks and subtasks, and by perceiving the finished opus as something that can be done in a number of steps. You plan time by allocating it in whatever lengths you find manageable to the tasks, sections, steps of the work.

Some writers don't plan at all. Or so I've been told. They just sit when and where they please, and let fall on the paper whatever comes. This is what I have heard, but I have had no experience of such writers, and I sometimes suspect they are as mythical as the unicorn and the mermaid. (If, as that most delightful of graffiti asserts,

"Ginsberg revises," then I add, nodding, "Henry Miller works from an outline.")

Anyway, I would at least admit that some writers plan work but not time; other writers plan time but not work; and a third group plan both. And there are writers in all three groups, I have no doubt, who leave behind them a litter of discarded and failed plans at every turn.

There is nothing I like better than having the idea for something — let's say a short, humorous essay or a 1,500-word story — spring fully formed into my mind at an opportune moment so that I can simply leap to my desk, sit down, and get it all on paper without further ado. However, this sort of thing doesn't happen very often, at least not to me. I'd estimate that in twenty-odd years of writing I've written perhaps a dozen pieces in that fashion, no more. Everything else has taken some kind of planning: ideas needed organization, stories too long to be written at a sitting had to be blocked out into sections, schedules had to be followed in order to meet deadlines, and so on. It would be idyllic never to have to plan, but the writer who never needs to plan may also be the writer for whose work no editor, producer, or publisher is ever waiting.

If I am at all an expert on planning, painful experience rather than astounding success has brought it about. I am learning, however, and I think I can share with you what I have learned, which is basically this: *Begin by understanding the purpose of planning.*

The purpose of planning is *not* to hem you in, *not* to make you toe the line and meet schedules, *not* to inhibit all those impulses to follow sudden inspirations. The purpose of planning is to eliminate dithering, to free you of small daily decisions and to disengage your mind from concerns other than the one immediately at hand. The purpose of planning is also to assure you, before you begin, that you actually have something substantial worth writing. If you are an impulsive writer constantly beginning with great ideas that somehow dwindle away into nothingness and have to be abandoned, you may need to plan your work, simply to find out whether you have anything there to write. If you can't put the gist of it into some kind of outline or statement, maybe you don't *have* any gist; and it's better to find this out before you start page one rather than after you finish page twenty.

But all plans should be flexible and roomy. Work should be planned flexibly enough to allow the mind to play and move freely. Time should be planned flexibly enough to allow for diversions and delays. Rigidity and creativity are incompatible. Cast-iron chapter plans and cast-iron schedules for writing them are fine — if you happen to be a talented computer. If you are human, something closer to Playdoh or Silly Putty would be more suitable.

The virtue of planning is that once you have an outline or a schedule made, you can give full attention to the page in front of you, knowing that you have allocated and organized properly for the pages still to come. In other words, plan ahead — and then stop looking ahead.

Finally, don't over-plan. Remember, the "best laid schemes o' mice and men gang aft agley" — and they take up too darned much time, besides. Compulsive planners (and I should know) sometimes pour so much time and energy into planning that they have little left for the work itself.

Well, back now to Chapter Nine. A little agley, but no harm done. That's what a flexible plan is for.

17

Joy on Wheels

L AST night was library night for us. We drove down-
town in a warmish drizzle and came back an hour and
a half later with several armloads of books. We piled them
all in the middle of the round oak table where we eat all
our meals, poured cups of cocoa all around, and sat down
in an amiable literary circle, reading bits and passing the
books about to everyone but Robin, whose management
of a cup of cocoa is still not expert enough to be trusted
near an open library book.

I had spent most of my time in the Children's Room,
where no book is higher than my nose and most are down
by my knee somewhere, so that I crept about in a crouch-
ing shuffle rather as if I were practicing some kind of
jungle warfare tactics. But I had found a wonderful *Ra-
punzel* in German, with a satisfyingly witchy witch making
off with the howling infant under her arm; Marie Hall
Ets' classic *In the Forest;* Taro Yashima's *Umbrella,* with
its unforgettable onomatopoetic raindrops, falling

Bon polo
bon polo
ponpolo ponpolo
ponpolo ponpolo
bolo bolo ponpolo
bolo bolo ponpolo
boto boto ponpolo
boto boto ponpolo

and Hugh Lofting's *Story of Doctor Dolittle.* For myself, I chose a half-dozen books, including a Gideon mystery by J. J. Marric, Randall Jarrell's *A Sad Heart at the Supermarket,* and Christopher Morley's *Parnassus on Wheels.* I also picked up what I call "A Rotten Novel" — it shall remain nameless — for every so often I get this craving to read (what else can I call it?) a rotten novel, and I indulge myself. Anyway, I brought this Rotten Novel home and read it in two sittings, half before bedtime and the other half after breakfast. It wasn't any better than I expected it to be, but it did have one marvelous moment in it, when its heroine wished she had a trashy novel to read. With great difficulty — and I succeeded only because of my high moral code regarding library books — I restrained myself from writing in the margin, "Lady, you're *in* a trashy novel!" Aren't libraries marvelous? You can borrow from them not only the books you can't afford to buy, but also, now and then, one of those books you wouldn't dream of spending the money on even if you had it.

I love public libraries. And this was one of those good nights at the library when the shelves were crammed with books I wanted to take home. I even spent a few tantalizing moments watching a woman almost taking one of *my* books off the shelf. I kept wondering what it would be like to pluck it off myself and hand it to her, grinning to match the dust-jacket photo. But I didn't, of course, and she left me there, leaning against Bennett Cerf. I am actually pretty shy.

Anyway, it was a good night at the library and I stopped extracting books from the shelves only when I could not stagger around any longer with those I already had. And yet — and yet I missed something, and I've been missing it for some time now.

What I miss is the bookmobile. Big libraries in big cities are fine and exhilarating places, but I have a passion for bookmobiles, and last night, despite all the riches at my command, I was suddenly nostalgic, thinking of Sara and Joe and the Washoe County Bookmobile.

One excellent thing about a bookmobile is that when you've chosen your books, you can be pretty sure you've chosen exactly what you wanted most out of all the books that were there. I could always, for example, look at every children's book in the Washoe County Bookmobile — something I certainly didn't do last night at the library, although my leg muscles seem to think I did. And if ever there was some special thing I wanted and couldn't find, why, Sara and Joe would bring it on their next trip around. Not only that, but when I checked out my books, Sara would often reach down and pull out something she'd brought along because she thought I'd like it. And she was usually right, too.

Then there's the informal atmosphere and the lively conversation — for who can be standoffish in a place the size of a bookmobile? — and (Robin would add at this point) the Life-Savers and chocolate-coated raisins that always seemed to be available around the driver's seat. But none of these things explains why I get a lump in my throat whenever I see a bookmobile. For I am truly and embarrassingly *sentimental* about bookmobiles — the way I am about merry-go-rounds and symphony orchestras and baby goats — and while I certainly don't know all the reasons why, I think I uncovered one reason when I brought home *Parnassus on Wheels*.

Now, *Parnassus on Wheels* isn't about a bookmobile. That is, it isn't about a library on wheels; it's about a bookshop on wheels. But that is a minor quibble. *Parnassus on Wheels* was first published in 1917, and I suppose

I read it in about 1933, when I was eleven, just old enough to find the love story touching. This afternoon, I read it again.

It's not by any means a great book. By today's standards it's pretty corny stuff. But Roger Mifflin, the red-bearded, five-foot-four, hundred-and-twenty-pound itinerant bookshop proprietor — why, he's obviously a Real Hero. He is just the sort of man to appeal to me, for all my life I have been devoted to men like Vladimir Nabokov's *Pnin*, like the feckless hero of Bernard Malamud's *A New Life;* like Moonbloom of Edward Wallant's *The Tenants of Moonbloom* — offbeat, downbeat, undersized, and yet somehow triumphant — and I must have daydreamed, I'm sure, of being swept off my feet by a small, feisty, bearded bookshop owner. Anyway, I suspect that some of the affection I had for *Parnassus on Wheels* and for R. Mifflin, Prop'r., has lingered through the years and attached itself to their modern counterparts.

I shouldn't say "modern," however, for the first bookmobile, so I've read, was put on the road in Washington County, Maryland, way back in 1905. I don't know how many bookmobiles there are now, but bless them all and long may they roll, bringing Hemingway on wheels, Beckett on wheels, Shaw on wheels, Erle Stanley Gardner on wheels, to all corners of the land. The best news I've had all month is that a bookmobile is coming! and will be stopping on Friday mornings at the school just across the freeway. Sara and Joe won't be there, but whoever it is, here's notice: I'll be there, damp-eyed and happy, library card in hand.

18

Butter by the Firkin

SEVERAL years ago, when we were living in Nevada, we found a trunk full of books in the desert. Because it was Nevada, both trunk and books were in fair shape and were promptly brought home to be added to our collections (of trunks and of books). (Whatever it is, we seem to be collecting it: trunks, books, rocks, shells, stamps, coins, keys, postcards, antique cameras, Indian baskets, old bottles, hunks of driftwood, and stereopticon slides.) Needless to say, we all had a fine time going through the old volumes before storing them away in cardboard cartons. I haven't looked at them recently, but I do remember particularly a book of fancywork projects which rejoiced in the title, *Dainty Work for Dainty People*. Another favorite was a thick book of dramatic recitations, complete with an illustrated catalog of gestures to be used for the expression of Joy, Grief, Supplication, Renunciation, Horror, Disdain, etc., with photographs of such performers as Edwin Booth and Mrs. Minnie Maddern Fiske. (When I say "old volumes" I *mean* old volumes!)

One of the books, however, we've kept out of storage. It's here on my desk: *The Elementary Spelling-Book*, by Noah Webster, L.L.D., "Being an Improvement on The American Spelling Book, The Cheapest, the Best, and the Most Extensively Used Spelling Book Ever Published." This is a posthumously-revised edition, brought out in

March of 1880 and copyrighted by Dr. Webster's then-
surviving children, Emily, Julia, Eliza, William and
Louisa. It is a small blue book, only about four inches by
seven, and while its 174 pages are brown, dry, and brittle
as the outer peel of a Bermuda onion, well, that was beginning to happen to *me* in Nevada, too, and I'm nowhere
near eighty-nine years old. It is, all things considered, in
pretty good condition.

The tone of the book is set by its frontispiece, an en-
graving of a buxom lady in classical dress who is leading
a barefooted child up a flight of stairs to a building with
KNOWLEDGE inscribed on its frieze, behind which rises a
domed structure on which is written FAME. Learn everything in this little book and you are on your way!

Well, I am ready — lead on! — for who can resist a
speller which lists, as on page 34, such words as gusset,
cosset, comfit, cumfrey, and shallop? Can you define all
five? — Quickly, now! (*Cumfrey* — ?) And who can resist
a speller with sample sentences like, "The farmer hatchels
flax; he sells corn by the bushel, and butter by the firkin."
(He does *what* to flax? And how much, pray, is in a firkin?
I had to go look it up: one-fourth of a barrel, if that's any
help to you, but how many of us ever see a barrel these
days, much less know how much is in one?)

I picked up a modern speller for purposes of comparison. I opened it at random, and here is the sample sentence that met my eye: "She went to her counselor for
advice about her high school schedule." Is it possible that
that sentence will ever strike us with a pang of nostalgia,
as these do now? Listen:

"The linchpin secures the cart-wheel to the axletree."
"The little sister can knit a pair of garters."
"A mercer is one who deals in silks and woolen cloths."

"The streets, houses, and shops in New York are illuminated by gas lights."

"I will try to get a mess of peas for dinner." (Once, when I used the word *mess* like that, my children exclaimed in utter consternation!)

"Shut the gate and keep the hogs out of the yard."

But if I sigh over the evocation of rural, pre-electric America, I must also take note of a somewhat less advanced sociology:

"We punish bad men to prevent crimes." (Those were the simple days!) "Savage nations inhabit huts and wigwams." (No nations are savage now, just underdeveloped or *emerging*.) "It is almost impossible to civilize the American Indians." (Tsk!)

And there was nothing, then, to keep these statements out of a school textbook: "God ordained the sun to rule the day; and the moon and stars to give light by night. . . . God governs the world in infinite wisdom; the Bible teaches us that it is our duty to worship Him. . . . The devil is the great adversary of man. . . . The heathen are those people who worship idols, or who know not the true God."

Even more prominent than religion is the attack mounted on demon rum; what a nation of sots we must have been, to have inspired it! "We pity the slavish drinkers of rum. . . . The drunkard's face will publish his vice and his disgrace. . . . Intemperance is a grievous sin of our country. . . . Liquors that intoxicate are to be avoided as poison. . . . Rum, gin, brandy, and whisky are destructive enemies to mankind. They destroy more lives than wars, famine, and pestilence. . . . Drunkards are worthless fellows, and despised." On and on they go, sometimes two to a page. Jill's speller, on the other hand, hasn't a word in it about pot or LSD; I glanced at it again and came up with "It was altogether impossible to follow the committee's suggestion."

But the words themselves are what I'm really in love with. The modern speller lists words alphabetically, a list for A, another for B, and so on, with occasional lessons on "demon" words, ance-ence errors, homonyms, and so on. Dr. Webster, however, lists words according to number of syllables, placement of stresses, and other structural matters, a method which turns his lists into virtual poems or chants. Listen to amber, member, limber, timber, umber, cumber, lumber, number; or botany, elegy, prodigy, effigy, ebony, energy, liturgy, infamy! Or how about cherubim, seraphim, martyrdom, idiom, javelin, ravelin, harlequin, myrmidon, lexicon, decagon, octagon, pentagon, heptagon, hexagon, polygon, champion, pompion! (Ravelin — ? *pompion* — ?) And then there's calomel, citadel, infidel, sentinel, mackerel, cockerel, codicil, domicile, daffodil and (of course!) alcohol.

I could go on (baboon, buffoon, dragoon, raccoon, doubloon . . .), but I do want to tell you that I finally found cumfrey in our abridged *Oxford English Dictionary* — *Symphytum officinale,* a vulnerary plant — but the OED spells it comfrey; take your choice. As for pompion, it turned up handily in one of Dr. Webster's sample sentences, "Pompions are now commonly called *pumpkins,*" so it was out of date even then. And ravelin? That's some kind of fortification made with embankments. Let's see — you hatchel flax with a hatchel, which is a thingumajig with teeth on it; and there are thirty-one and a half gallons to a barrel, so there must be nearly eight to a firkin.

We have much to thank Dr. Webster for. Not only did he spend twenty years working on his dictionary — during which time the income from the little speller supported his family, even though his royalties were less than one cent per copy! — but he also found time, while writing a two-volume history of epidemics and pestilential diseases, a book on the rights of neutral nations in time of war, a history of the United States, and a number of other things, to agitate successfully for better copyright laws. "A man who saves the fragments of time will accomplish a great deal in the course of his life." (*The Elementary Spelling-Book,* p. 116).

Actually, I'm not interested in Dr. Webster's speller because of any passion for spelling *per se.* I am inclined to agree with linguist Robert A. Hall, Jr., who points out that ". . . in earlier times there was considerably more latitude in the use of alternate spellings such as *smoak* or *smoke, cloak* or *cloke, cloathes* or *clothes.* No harm was done by the existence of such alternatives, nor would it be done at present." In fact, any language spelled as abominably as English is spelled probably deserves every misteak it gets.

But the little speller is delightful, nevertheless. Oh, those lovely words!

Cinnabar . . . provender . . . ambergris . . . porringer . . . parapet . . . summerset . . . hortulan . . . philomel . . .

Hortulan — ?

19

The Secret of Success

LET'S put down here in black and white the one sure-fire secret of success.

No, I'm not going to say, "Hard work." You can work hard and nevertheless fail. People do it every day. I heartily recommend hard work, but I'd never recommend it as a sure-fire thing.

Actually, it's easy to succeed. The secret is this: All you have to do is aim low enough, and *success will be yours*.

Perhaps we shouldn't call it a secret. Many people know it and practice it faithfully. Many more practice it unwittingly. And as a principle it has some noted backers. Longfellow, for example, says, "Most people would succeed in small things if they were not troubled with great ambitions." Nothing could be truer, right?

There is nothing difficult about this kind of success. It is disastrously, sinfully easy, and the temptation it offers is almost unavoidable. I have succumbed to it many times and for periods as long as half a year or more, during which periods I have been completely "successful" selling 100% of what I've written — instead of the 60% which is my overall rate so far. All I did was to write exactly what I knew I could sell, taking no risks, attempting nothing beyond my already demonstrated powers, and trying nothing new. What could be more economical and more prudent? I wasted no time and not even any postage. During the best of these periods I sold fifteen scripts in a row.

Every shot was a bull's-eye, and what more could you want?

Well, you might want, for example, a target farther away than four feet.

So you may, if you wish, take careful stock of your confirmed and pre-tested abilities, adjust your aim accordingly, and thus make prudent plans for a completely successful writing career.

I have other plans.

For there is one big trouble with this secret of success. It stunts your growth. Great ambitions may be troubling, but small successes "can become, in fact, a cozy trap, a comfy, padded, reassuring dead end; the small succeeder goes through life never failing at anything, for he knows exactly what he dares to attempt and thus achieves one cheap victory after another." The quote is from me — I've said it before and I haven't found any reason to change my mind since.

A string of small successes which have not stretched or even nudged the limits of your capacities is in itself a kind of failure; and there is something especially sad about failing not because you fell short of a distant and arduous mark, but because you were too timid and prudent to set your target where, to be sure, you might have missed it, but where you could at least have been truly proud to have hit it. (Please note, however, I am not talking about sending manuscripts to ridiculously unsuitable markets, shipping the *Jack and Jill* story off to *Redbook*, I'm talking about the aim you take when you sit down to write in the first place!)

Educators have a word for the student who may be doing acceptable work but who never works up to his own capacity; he's an underachiever. An underachiever: that's Rembrandt painting pretty flowers around the edge of a china plate, Dylan Thomas writing greeting card sentiments — and *you,* if you're not always pushing your target a little farther away, sometimes completely out of range.

I think I hear a voice saying, "Move my target? I haven't even hit it *once* yet!" But please, don't go away. Your first success will come, one of these days. And be warned: welcome as it will be, it can corrupt you. It can fence you in. It can do it so prettily that you hardly notice what's happening and you settle down cheerfully inside the little white pickets without a second glance at the big world beyond. How wonderful that *The Sunshine Basket* took your poem, "My Chickadee"! Three months later you have written a verselet about every bird you know, short of the turkey vulture, the white-rumped shrike, and the flammulated screech owl. Absurd? But I have spent too much time as a small succeeder (albeit on a slightly less absurd level) to laugh more than briefly. After success, failure is hard to take, and our reluctance to encounter it can lead us into excesses of both prudence and repetition.

Peace of mind, of course, will be the reward of those who nod wisely with Longfellow and content themselves with small successes. And we must all, sooner or later, come to some kind of terms with our limitations; I know *I* am no potential Shakespeare, and most of you must eventually recognize something of the sort about yourselves. But unmitigated peace of mind can be a fairly stupefying condition, and I hope that even when you have settled for what you are, you will be troubled by ambitions at least great enough to make you a trifle imprudent now and then.

So when I wish you success, I wish you the best, most satisfying kind of success — the hard-won kind. As for me, I plan to try some things I'm not at all sure I can do. I plan, in short, to dare to fail.

20

What Makes a Pro a Pro?

IN almost every realm of activity except perhaps love, tennis, and a few other sports, most amateurs have a hankering to become professionals.

A professional writer is, by what I suppose to be the most usual definition, one who makes his living from his writing. However, this definition is not as clear-cut as it appears to be. A writer may make $2,000 a year and by Spartan living make it cover all his expenses. Another writer makes $2,000 a year but blows it all each summer on foreign travel, while he lives on the income he gets from teaching English to college freshmen. Still another writer makes $2,000 but happens to be female and married to a man who makes $15,000 a year. Is only the first writer a professional?

(And there is also the case of J. Paul Getty, the multi-millionaire who writes for *Playboy*. I don't know what Mr. Getty makes from his writing, but it could certainly be more than enough to let our freshman English teacher leave the classroom and our lady writer leave her husband, if she wishes. Is *he* a professional writer? He certainly doesn't make *his* living writing, even though he may make enough for a number of Spartan writers to survive on handily.)

If at one end of the scale you have the writer who derives 100% of his income from writing but lives on spaghetti and what I call Soup Stojana (in honor of a room-mate I once had who knew how to make this gourmet dish out of a few aged tatters of vegetable peel, a moldy rind of cheddar, and a number of spices), and at the other end you have a millionaire who derives some microscopic fraction of his income from writing; well, you can see that "making a living" certainly won't do as a criterion by itself. As a matter of fact, Mr. Getty, with his name on the masthead and his articles prominently featured and well written, could put up a good claim to being a professional writer even if he gave his writing away — which, for all I know, he may do. And, for a complete contrast, we might assume that our Spartan spaghetti-eater is a thoroughgoing fifth-rater, selling thousands of pages to such low-paying markets that only by dint of incredible wordage does he manage to rack up his $2,000 a year.

Maybe money isn't a good criterion at all. My old Webster gives one set of definitions of *professional* based on financial gain, but another set, which is given first, has nothing to do with money. Included in this set is the definition, "characterized by or conforming to the technical or ethical standards of a profession." With that in mind, can we call a man a professional writer if he works at his writing as most professional men work at their professions, whether or not he earns his living at it?

I've always preferred this definition to any definition in terms of dollars. For one thing, it has allowed me to continue to call myself a professional writer even in those bad years in which the money I earned would barely have provided a reasonable living for a mongrel pup. And if you must know, by our first definition I have never *been*, strictly speaking, a professional writer. I didn't begin to write until after I was married, and, considering the way my income rises and falls (rather like the stock market and often just as mysteriously), I should very much hate to be thrown out into the cold and told to survive on it.

So I used to insist that a truly professional writer would have regular working hours; would keep adequate records; would be scrupulous about the physical condition of manuscripts he submitted; and would be reliable in matters of rewriting, cutting, proofreading, and meeting deadlines. (Mercy, what a prig!) A few missed deadlines and manifest unreliabilities of my own were enough to show me the light, of course. And besides, what about a writer who keeps no records, who writes on Monday from nine to noon, on Tuesday from one a.m. to four, on Wednesday from six p.m. to Friday, and not at all for the entire month of April or the year of 19—; who types as if wearing mittens but obviously isn't because he leaves dirty fingerprints on the margins (he has never learned to change ribbons with any proficiency, and neither have I); who refuses to alter a line or indeed a word; who misses half the errors when he reads proof; and who is always about a year and a half late — with works of sheer genius? His methods may be professionally horrifying, but who among us wouldn't like to fit that description — as long as those last few words are there?

Well, define it yourself to include yourself if you wish, but just remember: the word *amateur* has a very appealing etymology. There are distinct advantages in remaining somewhat of an amateur for as long as possible, especially if in becoming a professional you are tempted to place such a strain on your work as to press out all the joy and love, leaving only grim determination. From such a dismal post, all the Muses are bound eventually to flee.

I wonder if the happiest professionals aren't those who have managed to keep a little of the amateur in their makeup?

21

Thoughts While Jogging

THE alarm goes off like a Rebel Yell at 5:45 a.m. I have
the Loud-Soft control pushed as far over to Soft as
it will go, but what I need after twenty-two years of light-
sleeping motherhood is a clock that says "Psst!" or just
clears its throat discreetly like an English butler. Anyway,
after I stop vibrating, I get up and pad down the hall to
my oldest daughter's room. Ten minutes later, in sweat-
shirts and pants, we hit the road. The rest of the house
sleeps on.

There are no sidewalks here. The road snakes along the
hill, and at six in the morning it's safe to run on the faded
white line in the middle, if we wish. Cars are rare at this
early hour and the road too serpentine for excessive speed.

The sun crests the hilltop, strikes fires in valley win-
dows, melts a pale field to a luminous pool of gold. A
pheasant whistles. On the hillside above us, sheep move
and munch thoughtfully, bells tinkling. A few of them
lift their heads and look at us with insultingly mild curi-
osity.

On our first day out, I was winded before we reached
the first bend in the road, just below the old cemetery.
Now I can make it all the way to the baronial mansion
with the iron gates before I break to a walk. Polly tactfully measures her pace to mine and sometimes (tactfully?)

gets a stitch in her side. Then we walk, stoking our lungs with the cool, just-unwrapped morning air, until we are ready to run again.

Jill, who is younger and has reached that age at which nothing is potentially more mortifying than the behavior of one's parents, was horrified when I announced my intention of taking up jogging. "Out on the *road?*" she cried. *"What if someone sees you?!"*

I assured her that at six in the morning it was unlikely that anyone would be watching. Besides, most of the houses on our road are well above or well below it; only the mailboxes stand near the road. But at any rate, I said, I intended to go ahead with it, all risk of embarrassment notwithstanding.

Well, in one respect I was wrong. On our very first morning we were seen by two neighbors. We met first one gentleman and then, some ten minutes later, the other. Both smiled, greeted us, slowed down long enough to exchange a few words, and then went on their way down the road — jogging, both of them.

As for the occasional driver who passes us, well, it's hard to tell whether a smile from inside a car is patronizing, amused, or simply friendly. Never mind, I tell myself, the smiling driver can't smell the trees, can't hear the pheasant's whistle, misses the rustic sound of the belled sheep — and moreover, his arteries are hardening as he goes by. (Jogging has one great moral danger: it can make you insufferably smug.)

You can't talk much while jogging. At least you can't if you're my age and run short of breath after the first quarter-mile. A leisurely conversation is out of the question when I'm chugging along one-and-a-half yards behind my long-legged adolescent daughter. So I've been doing some thinking, instead, about jogging — and (it just dawned on me) about writing. My advice to beginners applies equally well to both activities.

If you want to be a jogger (or a writer), you must be unmindful of the smiles of passing motorists, the scoffing of friends and relatives, the embarrassment of progeny. There are those who are bound to say you're crazy. Depending on your age and circumstances, they'll suggest that you're too old to start, or that you're wasting your time, or that you'll never stick to it, or that you ought to get into some activity more immediately profitable. Or they may simply smile a knowing and enigmatic smile. Ignore them.

And when you jog (or write), you have to learn your own limits and set your own pace. Sometimes you'll be running, sometimes you'll be walking, and sometimes you may even stop and pretend to tie your shoe. Each day is different — and each jogger is different, too. If you start worrying about joggers who pass you when you're slowed to a walk, you're going to quit. Remember, you don't know where the other jogger started from, or how long he's been at it, or how often he comes out, or when *he's* going to slow down and walk. Jogging isn't competitive in the gross sense of the word; neither is writing. You compete only against yourself. But of course you still must learn to be a good loser on those days when you just aren't up to snuff.

You may remain a two-mile-a-day jogger all your life. Or you may find yourself turning into a long-distance runner. And it's easy enough to translate *that* into writing terms. But there's a major difference between jogging and writing. Jogging, apart from its salubrity, is always a round trip. All I do when I jog is eventually get back home again; I look at the view, smell the air, nod at the sheep, listen to the birds, and enjoy it all immensely, but I don't *arrive* anywhere.

When you write, however, steady does it. Two pages a day add up — unlike the jogger's two miles, they do not (necessarily!) repeat themselves. Of course you can tell yourself that if you jog two miles a day five days a week, in fifty-two weeks you've almost run from Reno to Salt Lake City; but you're really still stuck in suburban Sweatsock Junction. On the other hand, if you write two pages a day five days a week, in fifty-two weeks you'll have 520 pages — and some of them might even be worth keeping.

Above all, remember that the hardest part of jogging doesn't take place out on the road. It's not the muscle that hurts. It's not the dry throat (try chewing gum, that's what I do). It's not coming home tired and aching. It's not even being laughed at. The hardest part is getting up out of that warm bed an hour early and making it out the front door.

Think about it. Isn't that the hardest part of writing, too? It's not the pounding on the typewriter, not the searching for the right phrase, not the aching head and weary seat. It's that terrible moment — that 5:45 a.m. of the soul — when you have to make yourself sit down and do it.

No more excuses: Hit the road!

P.S. Ask your doctor first, of course — but jogging's great for the much-too-sedentary writer. This morning it even inspired me to a piece of writing.

22

Without Prospect or Retrospect

THE second time I read the Bhagavad-Gita, which was the morning after the night I read it the first time, I burst into tears. This occurrence is in itself of no consequence and does not bear directly on the discussion that follows here — I have burst into tears on innumerable occasions, moved by cosmic sorrows and unutterable sentimentalities alike — but what is relevant to my topic is that I happened to record the event in print, thus endowing it with a certain amount of permanence. So it was that just the other day I received a letter which put to me the following question: *"How many times have you moaned in the night about making that confession?"*

I could reply that insomnia is not on my list of complaints and that I habitually fall asleep much too quickly to be found moaning about anything. However, such a response, even though true, is evasive; and besides, I haven't the least desire to close the subject without saying my piece upon it, as follows:

Any writer who deals in *self* has no business moaning in the night about confessions made in print. Or, conversely, anyone who thinks he might moan in the night about confessions made in print had better not be a writer, at least not one who uses the pronoun "I" and means it. He had better write technical manuals or brochures for Sunset

Acres Retirement Ranchettes, anything where the self is kept at more-than-arm's-length so that the pen reveals nothing.

As for me, I can't keep my clamoring self out of my writing. But I certainly refuse to be haunted by reproachful spectres of things I said several years ago — or even last month. I try to tell it the way it is *when* it is, which means that my thumb-mark, as Llewelyn Powys puts it, is on every page; and if my thumb-mark betrays me so that I cannot deny that I was messing about with a particular pot of jam at such-and-such a time, well — I *did* weep over the Gita, and for all I know, I might do it again. I haven't tested myself on it recently.

What I have been reading recently, without tears, is a battered little copy of Emerson's essays. It has a broken spine and was once dropped open-face-down in the mud, but what Emerson has to say is neither spineless nor muddy. "Speak what you think now in hard words," he says, "and to-morrow speak what to-morrow thinks in hard words again, though it contradict everything you said to-day," and, continuing in this imprudent vein, he exhorts himself: ". . . let me record day by day my honest thought without prospect or retrospect" — an admirable precept from which I have taken my text and title.

No, I do not moan at night. On the contrary, I am only sorry I haven't managed to get more of my fallible and erratic self recorded on the spot. For, like Henry Miller, "Immediately I heard my own voice I was enchanted . . ." and can you imagine Henry Miller moaning in the night over something he's written? The writer who is enchanted with his own voice is wrapped up in what he's saying right here and now; he has no time to look forward or backward, to brood over how a statement may look ten years from now, to check on whether it agrees or disagrees with something he said ten years ago, or to watch for inadvertent and treacherous thumb-marks.

Self-betrayal doesn't bother such a writer at all, for *self* is what he's in the business of betraying. Does Norman Mailer moan in the night? I don't know Mr. Mailer, but I doubt it. And look at the thumb-marks on every page of his account of the march on the Pentagon, *The Armies of the Night* — ! The whole thing is one magnificent big paw-print; and that, in my opinion, is one reason it is such good reading.

Of course, if what you are engaged in putting on paper is not yourself but a carefully constructed image, then you *will* moan in the night; I guarantee it. We all do create images; we all play roles. But the key phrase here is "carefully constructed," and any image, any role that has to be built with meticulous care is too full of hazards for someone who likes to write the word "I" with cheerful insouciance and egotistical frequency.

Emerson, speaking of that foolish consistency he felt not worth cultivating, says that no man can violate his nature anyway, for "A character is like an acrostic or Alexandrian stanza; read it forward, backward, or across, it still spells the same thing." Which means, I think, that if you are supremely cautious in what you write, hoping to avoid all betrayals of naïveté, ignorance, sentimentality, wrongheadedness, et cetera, and hoping thereby to appear consistent, infallible, and wise, you will wind up looking not infallible and wise but only consistently *cautious*. And that, of course, is exactly what you will have been. (If you like the image, fine, but name me a great man — writer, statesman, scientist, or whatever — who achieved greatness because he was cautious. Caution is fine for crossing streets, handling other people's money, that sort of thing, but as a guiding principle and overall life style, it has really very little to recommend it.)

No one is under any sacred obligation to bare his soul and reveal all his vices, weaknesses, and secret longings to his readers. I certainly don't feel compelled to tell all. For one thing, I write mainly about writing, books, and domestic trivia — occasionally about larger ideas — and there are whole areas of my life and thought which have been, so far, irrelevant to this subject matter. Maybe I'll get around to them later, maybe not. At this moment I am still trying to figure out why I should moan about confessing my tears over the Bhagavad-Gita — hardly a searing revelation!

I'm not making a pitch for absolute (and probably impossible) honesty in writing about yourself. In fact, I find nothing particularly appalling in Henry Miller's statement, "I invent, distort, deform, lie, inflate, exaggerate, confound and confuse as the mood seizes me." So tell lies, if you want to, or be self-effacing and reticent, if that is what comes naturally to you. But whatever you do, be prepared to do it "without prospect or retrospect," because if you don't, you are either going to be so cautious that you'll never say anything worth listening to, or else you are going to be so miserable that you'll wish you'd never said anything at all.

23

I Remember a Bigger Teddy Bear

OUR number four son left this morning to go out into the world to seek his fortune. (Well, no, not exactly to seek his *fortune* — kids don't seek fortunes these days, at least not the kids I know; they seek meaning and involvement. Money was about the last thing on his mind, I'm sure.)

Anyway, he left on a Greyhound bus, taking with him our blessing and five suitcases, two of them filled with books, two with climbing and caving gear, and one with his small and shabby wardrobe. (He buys his climbing gear from a topnotch supply house managed by a member of the U.S. Everest team, but he insists on procuring his clothing at the Salvation Army Thrift Shop.)

When his older brother left for Europe a couple of years back, he took with him his copy of Poe's *Complete Tales and Poems*, one of my two copies of *Walden*, his antique flute — and no pajamas. No room for pajamas, he said.

But Cam did not go to a foreign land or into the wilderness. He's gone to Berkeley and has an apartment with friends waiting for him.

"There are lots of books in Berkeley," I said, as he began scanning the bookshelves in my room.

He knew that already. It was, in fact, one of the reasons he wanted to go there. All those bookstores — ! Even I

94

was sighing with envy, remembering my long-ago, foot-loose student days on Telegraph Avenue.

"I know," he said. He picked out a book. "May I take this?"

It was my *Collected Poems of Robert Frost*. My favorite high school teacher had given it to me when I was seventeen, and that was a long time ago, almost a quarter of a century before Frost died. I was going to say something: *I didn't know you cared that much for Robert Frost*. But I held my tongue.

He took his own books, too — books on caving and mountaineering, a guide to the High Sierra, the beautiful Sierra Club book, *On the Loose*. (You don't know *On the Loose*? Find it! Buy it! Read it! It's an unusual book; furthermore, it has a quotation in it that has joined the ranks of my favorites, and I certainly never thought I'd treasure a quote from Steve McQueen: "I'd rather wake up in the middle of nowhere than in any city on earth.") But he also took from our shelves Konrad Lorenz's *King Solomon's Ring*, two books by Bertrand Russell, *The Fall* by Albert Camus, George Orwell's *1984*, Darwin's *Origin of Species*, and a dictionary of geographical terms.

I looked carefully at what he had been piling up. There was my *Wolves of Mt. McKinley* by Adolph Murie (just as my husband is an otter-fancier and our middle daughter a hippopotamus-enthusiast, I have this passion for wolves; was this Berkeley-bound son planning to join me?) . . . and the same copy of *Walden* that had accompanied his brother to Europe and back home again . . . that self-same brother's selfsame Poe . . . and for some reason (suspicion nibbled at me) his father's ancient copy of *The Maylay Archipelago*, by Alfred Russell Wallace, Darwin's contemporary and a discoverer, independently, of the theory of natural selection. *The Malay Archipelago* — ?!

It occurred to me then that of course it did not matter that there are plenty of books available in Berkeley. These books were important because they were these books — and these specific copies, not a brand-new *Walden* or a Wallace, if he could find one, from some secondhand bookshop down Telegraph Avenue. These were *our* books.

And I began to realize that he was choosing our favorite books as much as his, and I wondered — if he'd dared, would he have taken one of his youngest sister's as well? (What a dead giveaway it would have been if he'd set out with a copy of *Bedtime for Frances* or *Where the Wild Things Are* tucked into his luggage!)

Do you suppose he'll read them all, I wondered, the ones he hasn't read already? I've been thinking about this all day, and I have the feeling that those books are less important to him as something to read than as something already read and treasured by the rest of us; that they are symbols of what we are, reminders of our family values and our attitudes toward the world, parts of a life shared — pieces of home.

He left behind his antique bottle collection and his little old Teddy Bear, Tim. Yes, he still has Tim — a Teddy Bear about seventeen years old, his original eyes long ago replaced with buttons from my sewing basket, his embroidered smile repaired.

"I don't know what I'd do if anything ever happened to this Teddy Bear of mine," he said, bringing Tim into the living room. (This is, I inform you, a young man who has climbed Mt. Popocatepetl and once spent ninety-six hours deep underground in a cave.)

His next-older brother, who had dropped in to say good-bye and possibly to check on the extent of the book raid, looked at Tim. "I thought you had a *big* Teddy Bear," he said. "I remember a bigger Teddy Bear."

"No," I said, "you remember a smaller brother."

He's gone now. The best of the bottles are on glass window shelves in the living room, and Tim is sitting on his bureau.

Take good care of those books, boy.

(Take good care of that boy, books!)

24

An Unbeatable Combination

O NE bright summer day a long, long time ago, my husband and I and two of our boys — the only ones we
had then — set out in a small boat from Friday Harbor,
Washington, our destination being Vancouver Island,
British Columbia. The boys were three and two; and there
was another boy, not quite ready to be born, who made *me*
not quite an able seaman.

To be honest, I wouldn't have been an able seaman
even without my handicap. As for my husband, he had had
one practice run with the vessel, and that was the extent
of his experience.

It was not a long voyage we had ahead of us. And all
was serene — sky of blue, sea of green — until we passed
through Speiden Channel and out into the more open
waters of Georgia Strait. Then, though the sun still
beamed and the sky was as innocently blue, the swells
became greater, the boat began to rear and plunge as she
met the waves, and suddenly we found ourselves fighting
the sea.

Everything in the galley began to slide, first one way,
then the other. The door to the head would not stay shut,
but banged back and forth. Awkward at best, I lurched
about perilously, and the two little boys turned pale and
green and crawled into their bedding in the forecastle to
escape. Up we reared, down we plunged, water breaking

over the bow. Turning back was impossible, because we simply didn't know how; we felt sure we would have been hit broadside, swamped and sunk, had we tried. So we tacked (I *think* you call it that) all the way to the Canadian shore, where, when we finally got in behind the breakwater at Sidney, we discovered what we would have known before we reached Speiden Channel, had we possessed a radio: that warnings had gone out long before, that the fishing fleet had all put in to harbor, and that nothing was afloat but the Coast Guard — and us.

How had we made it? Why, with an unbeatable combination.

"All you need in this life," said Mark Twain, "is ignorance and confidence, and then success is sure."

This is, however, no testimonial to the virtues of such witless courage. It would have been a sad story and I wouldn't have lived to tell it, had we foundered and gone down. The risk was unnecessary. We didn't need to get to Sidney on that particular day; the next day would have done just as well. People who set out in small craft without the least notion of what they're sailing into are less brave than they are stupid. We, assuredly, never did it again. And by the time we were safely moored, moreover, our confidence was rather mangled and our ignorance illuminated with considerable hard-won knowledge.

No, I will not speak a single word on behalf of ignorance where such hazardous undertakings are concerned. Running small boats, climbing mountains, flying planes, exploring caves — these are not occupations in which ignorance is in the least an advantage. But in other contexts there seems to be something to be said for the ignorance of which Mark Twain spoke.

For when it comes to writing, believe me, there are many times (perhaps as many as there are times I sit down to this typewriter) when I sorely wish I had my youthful ignorance back again.

It was a lot easier when I was ignorant to roll that first sheet of paper into the machine with a flourish and type, grandly, a title and my by-line. The first time I started writing a book, the words "Chapter One" didn't send a chill down my spine as they do now. I never — in effect — turned on the radio to check on the marine weather report. I just set out, willy-nilly, ignorant and confident, and — for this is the saving grace — full of young energy.

The process of using up one's ignorance in such matters is a painful one. And as ignorance is worn away by the abrasions of experience, the foolhardy, idiot bravery of the ignorant has to be replaced by cold courage.

Cold courage is the kind you need when you know what is ahead, when you know how hard it will be, how much energy you have, and how little you dare to waste. The very young often feel free to squander, as I did, and are not devastated when they must leave a capsized vessel in midpassage and swim for shore. Later, unfortunately, we all begin to feel the pressure of time; we hope to use our energies wisely, finish what we begin, and always reach the shore still at the helm. For that kind of undertaking, our risks must be calculated and not stupid, and we check everything out before we begin.

Sometimes it is tempting to take no risks at all. We end up not with cold courage but with tepid caution. And if ignorance leads you into hazard, an excess of wisdom can keep you in port indefinitely, or moving through such shallow and stagnant waters that you will ultimately run aground and will never have another adventure from the age of thirty-nine on.

Cold courage is hard to summon up, much harder than the hot, spur-of-the-moment bravery that is half lunacy.

There is an element of queasiness in it, and if your manuscript promises to be of any considerable length, you know full well that before the last page is proofread, chances are you will be not merely queasy but definitely nauseated. The amount of hard, grubby, carbon-smudged, blue-penciled, crumpled and thrown-across-the-room work that has to be endured during the course of a long piece of writing is really incredible.

"Seasickness is very anti-romantic," says Sir Francis Chichester. But how exhilarating and yes, romantic it was to watch him and *Gipsy Moth IV* making it alone around the world! Meanwhile, at the rail, Sir Francis (and he was 65) was having trouble keeping his breakfast down.

In some ways writing, like sailing around the world alone, makes a great spectator sport — romantic from a safe distance. I am coming into the most nauseating final weeks of something I am writing, but at least one friendly spectator, cheering me on, has already been talking of that triumphal bottle of champagne. Oh, I suppose I'll be ready for the champagne when the time comes, but right now, my thoughts run more to Dramamine.

And if you happen to need it, cold courage to you — and a strong stomach!

25

Castles in the Air

BACK in 1937, Bertrand Russell somewhat prematurely wrote his own obituary, setting the date of his future demise at June 1, 1962, an appointment which that grim Other Party missed, arriving about eight years late. For myself, I have no specific date in mind — although I'm not particularly interested in any time before the year 2001 — but I have often thought of writing my own obituary, even so.

It's not that I wish to reserve to myself the right to deliver that penultimate judgment, nor am I like a sulky, newly-punished child, envisioning his own funeral and the sorrow and contrition of the mourners. No, my motives are purely in the realm of self-betterment, as you will shortly see. However, I am too superstitious to tempt Fate — well, no, I'm not exactly superstitious, but I do cross my fingers when I go to the mailbox — and I can't help feeling that having everything in perfect order might, despite Russell's experience to the contrary, have an un-wished-for result.

So I haven't done it.

I have, however, drifted off to sleep while cheerfully and preposterously composing *Time* cover stories about my-self or while interviewing myself for *Playboy*. (I haven't yet figured out why I rarely get beyond the first paragraph and a half; it may be due to the fact that I have no truck with insomnia, but it may also be due to the fact that as an interviewee I am less stimulating than soporific.) But what, you may ask, have imaginary *Time* cover stories and mythical *Playboy* interviews to do with premature obituaries? And what has any of it to do with — what did I say? — *self-betterment?*

It all falls more or less under the heading of daydreaming, the utility of which I propose to discuss.

Daydreaming: a terrible waste of time, isn't it? Or is it? Well, let's omit obituaries as being a bit gloomy to contemplate, and we might as well throw out *Time* and *Playboy,* too — it's been my experience that they tend to get me off the track. But for those of you who may need it, I am going to prescribe some utilitarian daydreaming. The preliminary stipulation, however, is that these daydreams are to be committed to paper, not just allowed to drift through the mind while you are engaged in falling asleep or doing the ironing or riding the transit system to the unspeakable job whence cometh your daily ration of 16-pound bond. No, *you must write these dreams down.*

I have three categories of daydreams in mind: one — a fan letter you would like to receive; two — a review of your work you'd like to read; and three — your autobiography.

I've received some good fan letters over the past few years, and they do have an effect on me, other than swelling my head, that is. For when I'm writing, I often remember this one or that one (and some are engraved permanently in my memory) and say to myself, "Now, that is exactly the kind of response I want to get with this piece of work." Sometimes I even visualize the intelligent, perceptive (of course!) reader sitting down to write to me. This is not at all inhibiting, for I am not thinking of an editor who is coldly scrutinizing my work and deciding whether to buy it or not; I am thinking of somebody sitting somewhere with a cup of warmed-over coffee and my already-printed piece in hand, nodding in agreement, frowning in disagreement, and deciding to talk back to me a little. That is — the Perfect Reader!

However, when in this daydream you become the Perfect Reader and sit down to write yourself a fan letter, you must make it specific. Fan letters that say, "Wow! I think you're a great writer!" are fine for Instant Inflated Ego, but otherwise they don't help you much. What you have to know is just what bell you rang, what nerve you touched, what precisely you did to make someone exert himself to the point of writing a letter — and for most people, it is really quite an exertion.

The same requirement applies to writing a review. When in your daydream you become the enthusiastic reviewer, never mind the general superlatives which could describe anything from a new Vladimir Nabokov to the latest Ralph Nader attack on whatever most needs attacking. General superlatives create a warm glow — and wouldn't we all love to read them! — but the object of this exercise is not to make you drift off into a vague and rosy state of bliss; it is to make you more sharply aware of exactly what you're trying to do.

And of course, if you now understand fully the purpose of these daydreams, you will realize without my having to tell you that the fan letters and the reviews you write must be about *something you haven't finished writing yet* (or perhaps haven't even been able to *begin*, if you are as cold-footed as I — which no doubt a few of you are).

If you don't want to limit yourself to one work-in-progress (or work-stalled-and-in-trouble), you can try the more overall approach of the autobiography. Naturally, what

I mean here is the premature or prophetic autobiography, covering events starting roughly tomorrow morning or so, and going on for a year, let's say. What do you really wish could be written about your career at the end of the next twelve months? What do you really want to have happen?

It's remarkable how revealing this can be. I've often thought how nice it would be to be suddenly rich, but a funny thing happened when I sat down to write my projected autobiography. "On March first," I began, "I came into a mysterious legacy of half a million dollars. Immediately, I —" Immediately, I paused, pencil in air. Immediately, I paid the bills? I got our insurance policies out of hock? I blacktopped the driveway? I — uh — m-m-m —*quit writing*? Heaven forfend!

Well, the truth is, the money would be great and I could, with some thought, come up with all sorts of things to do with it, but it is a hundred times more *interesting* to me to imagine how I might earn even one-hundreth of half a million dollars (whatever that might be) by my own efforts and with the aid of this decrepit but beloved old typewriter. And, in case I hadn't already suspected it, I discovered that despite the fact that I write in order to earn money, I appear to be in the long run less concerned about the money itself than about how good my writing is and how closely my life and work conform to some image of myself which I carry deep within me. . . . "On March first, I laid aside the minor scripts that had been occupying my time, cut nonessential activities to the bone, warned my family that I would need their cooperation, and began work on my long-delayed novel. . . ."

Inane? A waste of time? If you are one of the fortunates who is already working full speed and never getting off the track, maybe so. But if you need to be reminded occasionally of what you're trying to do and where you're trying to go, of what you want to have written, and of what you want that Perfect Reader to think when he finally turns the last page, then for you such daydreaming is not as silly as it seems.

Why not just lay out a schedule, cold and tough? Why daydream? Well, for some of us a brutal agenda is more paralyzing than galvanizing; we respond better to daydreams, which invest our goals with a shining and beckoning allure. I cannot plan unless I have dreamed, and the dream must continue to shine behind the plans or else the plans will come to naught.

Remember what Thoreau concluded, near the end of *Walden*? "I learned this, at least, by my experiment: that if one advances confidently in the direction of his dreams, and endeavors to live the life which he has imagined, he will meet with a success unexpected in common hours. ... If you have built castles in the air, your work need not be lost; that is where they should be. Now put the foundations under them."

Nothing is achieved that was not first dreamed of.

26

Your Most Important Investment

NOT long ago we went to the bank to borrow some money. It wasn't that bills had risen up to engulf us; no wolfish creditors were howling at our door or following our troika with slavering jaws. What we were doing was borrowing in order to invest, our investment being the purchase of several acres of beautiful woods with a sweeping view of sea, sky, islands, and mountains.

Everybody knows that it costs money to borrow money, and one shouldn't do it lightly. And although it is at times unavoidable, I don't happen to think very highly of the practice of borrowing in order to buy *things*, things which begin to depreciate the minute you have them in your own possession. But when you have faith in something — be it an idea, a business project, an opportunity, or a piece of land of undoubted value — borrowing may be the only way to insure that it doesn't slip away from you. For such investments I wouldn't hesitate to borrow.

Do you know what your most important investment is? It's yourself.

Real estate is great, stocks and bonds are jolly, annuities are warm and cozy, and even a little savings account at five percent is a worthy place to put your spare cash if you are lucky enough to have any. But if you are a writer or are trying to become one, you'd be wise to look upon yourself as a fine place, in fact the *logical* place, to begin an investment program.

And like as not, in order to invest in yourself you'll be forced to borrow. In fact, you've probably already thought of it, though not in those terms at all, and may have given up the idea because the costs seem a little high, or because you're afraid of being turned down at the bank, in a manner of speaking.

Stop for a moment and think about it. Think about yourself as something which will increase in value if only given a chance. You are your own potential income-producing property. I advise you to invest in yourself, invest even if you must borrow in order to do it.

Borrowing money is for most of us probably the least of it, though every writer should have enough for supplies, postage, a typewriter or the use of one, and the basic references he needs — or bus fare to the library. You can no doubt borrow all you need from your own pocket, if you're willing to make choices and set priorities. If you're down to real penny-pinching, you can skip desserts and cut out smoking — and live to be a famous, *old* writer, into the bargain.

Borrowing time is more important and probably a lot harder. But the time is there, if you're willing to pay for it. Borrow some of it from sleep, but not most of it. Borrow more of it from the astonishing number of nonessential things you do every day. Borrow it from the television set. Is what's on there really worth the half hours and hours it eats up? Would you rather watch, or create something somebody else may eventually watch? Borrow from the kitchen, if you're a housewife. Will it kill them to eat TV dinners once a week, or even twice? Borrow from the iron-ing-board — a new wrinkle in a short story may be worth a lot of wrinkles in a tablecloth. Borrow from the PTA, from the club you belong to, from the lawnmower, and from the can of car wax.

This means, of course, that you must borrow the indulgence of others. For some of us this is the hardest loan of all to ask for, and it is the one we fear to have refused. But it is the most essential of all.

You must in effect beg the indulgence of others for using yourself for your own purposes. You must ask them to do without you, to overlook your absence at the meeting, in front of the television set, across the table, on the golf links. You must borrow their indulgence for those TV dinners, that wrinkled napery, a ragged lawn, a less-than-spotless family car. You must tell them you will not be available at such and such a time because you will be trying to write.

They may grumble. Families and spouses in particular tend to grumble. But the strange thing is that if you really have faith in this investment of yours, they may get caught up in that faith themselves and may be more willing than you think to lend you what you need. They may even astonish you by being enthusiastic.

(However, be warned — you may discover that you've been spreading yourself around mighty thin in places where you'll never be missed. I hope your ego can withstand such a disclosure, but even if it hurts, the time you gain is worth the blow.)

You are your own most important investment. You cannot borrow faith in yourself, or the courage to go ahead on the basis of that faith. These you must scrape up from your own inner resources. But if you do have faith in yourself, then invest in yourself — even if you must borrow heavily in order to do it.

27

Confessions of a Mole-Watcher

I OFTEN think of Mrs. Frances Trollope, Anthony's mother, who wrote tirelessly, day after day, while nursing a whole family of dependent invalids — not books as good as Anthony's, but at least books that kept them all fed and housed. Or I think of Dostoyevsky and his epilepsy, or of Kenneth Roberts and his ghastly plague of giant boils. Or of all those who have continued to write while coughing their lives away with consumption; of poets blind and humorists with little left to laugh at; of those who wrote in prison, in exile, or even in the madhouse.

But mostly I think of Mrs. Trollope.

Courage? — There's courage for you, to go on creating when so much has gone wrong!

Would I, I ask myself — would *I* be able to write from a wheelchair, write from a cell, write with the world darkening about me, write in pain, write under sentence of death?

Oh, I haven't the slightest doubt of it. Give me great adversity and I'll rise to it; I'll triumph over it. I'll fit incisor to incisor, molar to molar, nose to grindstone and gluteus maximus to chair seat, and I'll prevail. Unflinching determination will carry me through.

The trouble is, I can't cope with all these *trivial* interruptions.

On Monday my three daughters and I spent forty-five minutes sitting in a solemn, silent semicircle, watching a mole who was periodically pushing dirt up from his excavation under the lawn and sometimes showing his little pink nose.

On Tuesday one of our sons rescued a terrified young robin from our fiendish cat, and we all subsequently spent a day and a half first trying to feed him and then trying to encourage his timid parents to resume their natural obligations.

On Thursday an old feral cat turned up at the back door, sick and starved, and we have been tending him ever since, opening cans of sardines and tuna fish (meant for the children's school lunches) and combing his tangled and burr-knotted coat.

I don't know how to dispose of such matters. They occupy great amounts of my time, and there is no strength I can summon up with which to ignore them. Personal misery is quite another matter; I seem to be able to grit my teeth and scribble away hangnail and all, or keep Kleenex handy and go on doggedly writig eved whed I have a dasty code, but let someone tell me there's a weird bug on one of the roses or the Mama Swordtail is pregnant again and I'm lost.

I am, especially when animal life is concerned, the most distractible of writers. I often think it would be particularly wise for me to emulate Mrs. Trollope's habit of early rising. Anthony says she was always up long before anyone else in the family, and I daresay it wasn't even light enough to sit outside and watch moles, had she been so inclined.

But she was not so inclined. If she ever gave a thought to moles, it was doubtless to plot with a gardener for their extermination. I was reading about Mrs. Trollope the other day, in a biography with the title *The Indomitable Mrs. Trollope,* by Eileen Bigland. What I read indicated to me that there may be a dark side to her being indomitable, a side that fails to meet the eye in Anthony's autobiography. Anthony speaks of his mother's journey to America and her ill-fated attempt to establish an enterprise there that would save the family finances. (The enterprise failed dismally, but the book she wrote containing her impressions of this country, *The Domestic Manners of the Americans,* launched her on her career as a writer.) What Anthony doesn't say is that she left him and his father behind apparently without a qualm, dragged poor, sickly Henry about with her and deluded herself as to the "temporary" nature of his ill health, and stayed nearly four years. "The thought of leaving the twelve-year-old Anthony to the care of his irascible, intolerant father troubled her not at all," says her biographer. "He was the sturdiest of her flock and, one regrets to record, the child she loved least. Perhaps even then she recognized the latent power within him and instinctively resented it." Hm-m . . .

I came away from Miss Bigland's book wondering whether I should admire Mrs. Trollope's courage or deplore her insensitivity, applaud her fanatical devotion to the task of supporting her family, or suspect that there may have been just a little of the self-centered monster in her makeup. But then I thought, *Hold on, mole-watcher; maybe you're just trying to justify your own limitless distractibility.*

So I went back to read what that child she loved least had to say in his *Autobiography*:

> . . . my mother's most visible occupation was that of nursing. . . . There were two sick men in the house, and hers were the hands that tended them. The novels went on, of

course. We had already learned to know that they would be forthcoming at stated intervals . . . and they always were forthcoming. The doctor's vials and the ink-bottle held equal places in my mother's rooms. I have written many novels under many circumstances; but I doubt much whether I could write one when my whole heart was by the bedside of a dying son. Her power of dividing herself into two parts, and keeping her intellect by itself clear from the troubles of the world, and fit for the duty it had to do, I never saw equalled. I do not think that the writing of a novel is the most difficult task which a man may be called upon to do; but it is a task that may be supposed to demand a spirit fairly at ease. The work of doing it with a troubled spirit killed Sir Walter Scott. My mother went through it unscathed in strength, though she performed all the work of day-nurse and night-nurse to a sick household . . . for there were soon three of them dying.

No, she was not one to watch moles.

Frances Milton Trollope, 1780–1863; mother of Thomas Adolphus, Henry, Cecilia, Anthony and Emily; she wrote over one hundred books, *beginning* when she had already passed her fiftieth birthday. — Oh, yes, those of us with such flaws as incorrigible mole-watching are ever ready to hunt for black spots in the souls of the more prolific and less distractible. Surely a woman who could write a hundred books under such circumstances must be less *human* than I?

How I hate to be reminded, when I am inspecting weird bugs, tending robins, doctoring stray cats, and watching moles at work, that if I ever want to accomplish anything of note I had better learn to cleave to my typewriter! Or, perhaps, learn to write about moles?

At the very least, mole-watcher, be grateful that nothing more earthshaking than a mole is interrupting you.

28

Living with a Writer

BEHIND my typewriter and to the left of the postal scales on my big, messy desk, I keep a small collection of reference works. There's a dictionary, of course, and a thesaurus; Sir Ernest Gowers' *Plain Words* and H. W. Fowler's *Dictionary of Modern English Usage*; two anthologies of quotations; and Dr. Spock's *Baby and Child Care,* which we have almost — at last! — outgrown. Other things come and go: I see a Driver's Manual there at the moment, and a book of exercises in italic calligraphy, and also a torn half of an envelope, bearing a cryptic note from me to myself concerning some brilliant idea I had a couple of months ago. I just pulled it out and read it, and I cannot recall why I thought it was so scintillating. Perhaps it would help if I could make out all the words; when the cryptic is also totally illegible, all is lost.

But what I really wanted to tell you is that I recently added a new volume to the lot — new to me, that is. It's a musty old copy of *The Reader's Handbook of Allusions, References, Plots and Stories,* with Two Appendices, by the Rev. E. Cobham Brewer, LL.D., of Trinity Hall, Cambridge, published by Lippincott in 1891, recently reissued. This is a feast of a book, a pudding stuffed with all sorts of nutmeats and tidbits, over eleven hundred pages of everything from Napoleonic numerical curiosities to a note informing me that "to win the Strawberry Leaves" means to be created a duke — which I certainly didn't know before. There are, for example, six and a half pages of various entries on the subject of *trees*, such as "Tree of Knowledge," "Tree of Liberty," "Tree of Life," and "Trees noted for Specific Virtues and Uses." There are lists of giants and lists of dwarfs; there are all manner of lists. And of course there are entries on characters from Scott, Dickens, Shakespeare, the *Bible*, Beaumont and Fletcher; from Greek, Roman, and Norse mythology, and from the *Arabian Nights*. I don't think there's a completely dull page anywhere from Aaron to Zulzu — at least, *I* can always pick it up and open it at random and find something to amuse or enlighten me.

So it was while browsing in Brewer the other day that I ran across this intriguing entry:

> Wives of Literary Men. The following were *unhappy* in their wives: Addison, Byron, Dickens, Dryden, Albert Durer, Hooker, Ben Jonson, W. Lilly (second wife), Milton, Molière, More, Sadi, the Persian poet, Scaliger, Shakespeare, Shelley, Socrates, Wycherly, etc. The following were *happy* in their choice: — Thomas Moore, Sir W. Scott, Wordsworth, etc. The reader can add to the list, which will serve as a heading.

As a matter of fact, this reader cannot add to the list, not offhand and without research. But I'd like to hazard a guess that if I were to add to the list and did it at random and unselectively, the relative lengths of the two categories (seventeen *unhappy*, three *happy*) might remain constant; winding up with seventeen hundred unhappy choices and three hundred happy ones, or perhaps five hundred and sixty-one relatively contenteds to three thousand one hundred and seventy-nine miserables.

It would thus be possible to prove statistically that writers simply cannot choose wives. Persian poet, English playwright, Greek philosopher, it matters not which — the bulk of literary men are clearly incompetent in making uxorial choices.

Which is, of course, absolute nonsense.

Because the real meaning of that three-to-seventeen ratio is that if you get twenty writers gathered together, seventeen of them will probably be the lousiest husbands imaginable; did anyone ever ask Xanthippe what it was like to be married to Socrates? (Think about it.) And yes, the same goes for the wifely qualities of any collection of twenty female writers; canvass their husbands and you'll find the same thing, and marriage being a reciprocal business, that means three literary wives happy in their husbands and seventeen just waiting for enough royalties to finance a divorce.

I exaggerate, of course (slightly); and my statistics, like television ratings, are extrapolated from a limited and somewhat suspect sample. Nevertheless —

Nevertheless, I have long meant to write about the daily hazards, the grinding irritations, and the occasional terrors of living with a writer. I thought I'd interview members of my own family — they ought to know. It would be, then, an objective presentation. I'd keep myself largely out of it and simply put on record what they regarded as the most harrowing aspects of life with me.

But when my husband sat down the other day and began, in earnest, working on the book *he* is supposed to be writing, I decided to throw such secondhand objectivity out the window. So let us consider *my* list of the negative aspects of living with a writer, the things that *I*, playing writer's spouse for a change, found most distressing.

Briefly, they are:

Silence

> *Temper*
> *Gloom*
> *Loneliness*

(Xanthippe's list would be entirely different. This is my list. Anyway, I wouldn't have put Socrates on a list of "Literary Men" in the first place. That's Rev. Brewer's doing, not mine.)

SILENCE. The writer often demands silence, a condition which may be difficult to achieve. But more terrible than the silence he demands is the silence he inflicts: that ominous silence that begins when the clatter of the typewriter stops, and grows and grows until it bulges out of the room and fills the rest of the house. It's palpable — a sort of gray-colored bread dough, risen up over your head, and you have to walk through it. Nevertheless, you feign an errand to take you past the doorway of the room where the silence is being created. If the door is ajar, you look in with a quick sidelong glance, hoping to see the writer leaning back in his chair and reading his last page with satisfaction. Instead, he is hunched forward, fists at his temples, staring at the typewriter with a baleful eye. You start to tiptoe away, but you've made your move too late. "When's lunch?" he wants to know. And it is only ten forty-five. You nod and go off to the kitchen, but you keep listening. And when the grilled-cheese sandwiches are on the plate and the coffee poured, you stagger under a sudden burst of machine-gun fire. The typewriter — ! Still, "Lunch?" you ask. He looks at you blankly, consults his watch. "It's only eleven-fifteen! Let me finish this paragraph, at least."

Lunch, at eleven forty-five: grilled-cheese sandwiches, leathery and stone-cold.

TEMPER. There's not much to be said about temper,

except that getting out of its way is a good idea. Take the cat and the children with you.

GLOOM.   Temper is dangerous, but gloom lasts longer. It can eventually pervade the entire household. Even the cat looks gloomy; his whiskers droop. The tropical fish drift morosely in the tank and seem to be thinking of turning on their backs and dying. The children sulk. I don't know which is worse, temper or gloom, but I suspect gloom is.

Finally, LONELINESS.   Much has been written of the loneliness of the writer, the inherent loneliness of his task, the loneliness he must have and yet often finds unbearable. But there is a correlative loneliness: the loneliness of the spouse who cannot break into the writer's loneliness, who cannot really share but can only watch, cut off and helpless, from a lonely distance. It, too, can be unbearable.

I wish there were, but there is not, a simple set of rules to follow for living successfully with a writer. There is no way to know when to be sympathetic, when to be cheerful, when to be absent, when to be present, when to inquire, when to be silent. There is only this to be certain of: no matter what you choose to do, it is rather likely to prove to be the wrong thing.

If I counsel patience and forbearance, I'm counseling both of you. Remember, writer — it's often not much fun being your spouse; remember, spouse — it's often not much fun being a writer. But with patience and forbearance on both sides (and with your fingers crossed for luck), you may wind up in the company of the Scotts, the Moores, and the Wordsworths — that happy fifteen percent.

29

It's Push, Not Pull

IS it true that there are fewer would-be writers around who are burdened with naïveté and illusions than there used to be?

Some years ago, I used to get a remarkable number of letters from people who were staggeringly ignorant about writing, editing, publishing, the whole business of words-on-paper-for-sale. People sent me short stories (I use the term loosely) and asked me if I would please "polish" them so that they'd be ready for marketing. People sent me novels and expected me either to get them past the fresh-from-college First Readers and under the bifocals of the Senior Editors, or to hand them over to my agent. Moreover, my mother-in-law once reported to me that a friend had asked her how much it cost me to have my first book published. (Cost *me*?! Well, blood, sweat, tears, ink, time, yes — but money? No, never!)

In the last few years, I have run across fewer and fewer such people; still, it happens. The other day a letter came from an unpublished writer who wanted help. I don't mind giving help, if I can. But the help this unpublished writer wanted was for me to read his book and then conduct both him and it to an agent and/or a publisher. He didn't want to know whether his book was any good or not; he knew it was. All he needed, he was sure, was to get in somehow or other, to have a door opened and an introduction made. If he just knew the right people, there'd be no more rejections. What he wanted was *pull*, in other words, and surely I would have it, wouldn't I, even if in only a modest quantity?

In case any of you out there are contemplating the same gambit (with me or with anybody else) or are afflicted with the same illusion, please listen.

I don't know anybody. I never did know anybody. And even if I did know somebody, it wouldn't be likely to do you much good.

I put in several years, long ago, sending out and getting back, sending out and getting back, being slapped and turning the other manuscript, getting knocked down and lurching to my feet again, paling with nausea at the sight of my own repulsive handwriting on my own repulsive Manila envelopes day after day. (I'm sure that last is a phrase I've used before, but never mind — it's apt.) Then, after a few minor sales and a couple of prizes in a short-story contest, an agent came to me. I have him yet, blessed man, and he has stuck with me through moderately thick and mighty thin. He earns his ten percent, believe me he does, but he would be the first to admit that if I wrote rotten stuff he wouldn't be able to sell it. No agent can sell the unsalable. He may be able to think of markets you couldn't think of, he may be able to work a lot faster than you can work when you have to mail your stuff out from Nowhere Corners, he may know editors by their first names, and he may be able to negotiate better terms than you could negotiate for yourself, but he still cannot sell the unsalable. An agent may at times seem marvelous, but he isn't *magical*. And most writers, let me warn you, protect their agents with a ferocity even exceeding that of doctors' receptionists protecting their doctors. I am no exception.

Do I know any editors and publishers? Well, in the past

two decades I have lunched twice with magazine editors. I usually lunch alone, or with the cat, or with my husband, or with one or more of our numerous children. None of the foregoing has any influence in the publishing world. Usually, however, I forget lunch, because I'm up here at my typewriter and it's three o'clock before I remember it. And that is really the most profitable way to spend my lunch hour, for while those two lunches with those two editors were both very pleasant and all that, nothing came of them. I sold at no greater rate to either of those editors after those lunches than I had before those lunches. They still reserved — and exercised — the right to reject my work. Another time I had a couple of drinks and an elegant meal with a publisher — whose publishing house has never published anything of mine and probably never will.

What about contacts with other writers? Surely that could be helpful? Let's see — I'm counting, and I discover that I really *know* only two other writers, a Canadian poet and a very nice guy who writes books for young people. Do we help each other? Certainly, by cheering each other up now and then, and that's about all we can do besides buying each other's books. Influence? — we have none to wield.

Oh, I'm sure that if I knew Vladimir Nabokov and if Vladimir Nabokov scribbled "This is great stuff" across the top of a manuscript of mine, people at Viking or Putnam or Knopf or wherever would perk up and look. But if he were demented enough to do it as a personal favor to me (a likely story) and if my manuscript were really mediocre or worse (another likely story!), somebody at Knopf or Viking or Putnam would scribble underneath, "V.N. has lost his marbles." So much for influence. Nobody has ever exerted any on my behalf and I haven't any to exert on anybody else's behalf.

Jean Cocteau, on being asked whether he believed in

luck, replied that he certainly did, for how else could you explain the success of people you don't like? Well, you might explain it with *pull*, too. Luck and pull — they both do exist, you know; I'm not saying they don't, although I am inclined, on the basis of personal experience, to give much more weight to the former than to the latter. So pull exists (though I don't have it), and that much I'll concede. But I believe firmly and unshakably that although pull does exist, it is not basically the way the publishing world works.

How come, then, there are books not as good as yours in print? And some of them are written by well-known people, too; surely that's *pull*? True enough, mediocre books by famous people are not exactly rare. But they are not published because their authors have pull with publishers. They are published because their publishers figure that their authors have pull with the public. That kind of pull is known as *drawing power,* and it's what draws people to the bookstores and to the cash register. But it's not much good secondhand; it doesn't really rub off.

Some books are published because they're good, some because somebody thinks they're good, some because they conform to a current fad, some because they are written by "names." But most books are published because their publishers believe (sometimes mistakenly) that they will sell. Your problem is to get a publisher to believe that about your book. And despite the undeniable role of luck and even the possibility of pull, I have always had the odd and puritanical notion that for the most part, merit and persistence are what matter.

If you have a manuscript that's been making the rounds, don't kid yourself; people have been reading it, they really have, and any Good Housekeeping Seal of Approval I might put on it wouldn't make much difference. So when do you give up? When your faith in your own merit runs out, I suppose. There's no mystical number of rejections at which point I would categorically advise anyone to call it quits. Do you believe in what you've written? Is it good? Well, then, just keep on pushing it.

Push, not pull. That's the thing.

30

Fringe Benefits

I'VE been writing and selling for more than twenty years now. This morning, with the house quiet and a piece of work I don't quite want to tackle sitting on my desk, I've been casting my mind back over those years, fat and thin, and reminiscing.

If you ask a writer to choose his own favorite works, he will not always choose the ones the critics or the public have chosen. A writer's opinion of his own accomplishments simply does not coincide perfectly with the opinions of others. Thus we have poetry anthologies in which poets give their reasons (often almost apologetically) for choosing certain poems of their own for inclusion; and we have other poetry anthologies in which editors, selecting the "best" from the same poets, give *their* reasons (not so often apologetically!) for choosing quite another assortment.

But, critical assessments of a writer's work itself aside, there is another area of possible disagreement. Perhaps disagreement is not the right word; what it is is a matter of perception and inner knowledge. No one but the writer himself can know what moments have been the real high spots in his writing career. Oh, I suppose a Nobel Prize and a thirty-seven-week appearance on the best-seller list must be high spots for any lucky soul who encounters them — I wouldn't know — but let's move down the ladder a few rungs, to those less rarefied levels where I'll know what I'm talking about.

High spots. It's funny, but I can't remember the day I got the news of my first book sale — and I can't forget the day I received a fan letter from France and spent the whole day out in the sun-corner of the backyard, laboriously translating it, French not being one of my talents. I must have been exhilarated the first time I was paid a four-figure check for a story, but I had to look into my files just now to find out which story it was. I haven't forgotten, however, how pleased I was the day my daughter's kindergarten teacher produced a playlet I'd written for some of our family puppets, or the day I sold, for a very modest sum, a story based on something our son had done, and I was able to buy him a new red tricycle with my earnings. I know which story *that* was.

High spots! There was the day I received a letter from a young man serving a term in a state penitentiary, thus beginning a correspondence and a friendship that still endure. There was the time the New York Board of Education asked permission to mimeograph one of my stories. And how astonished I was to hear from the president of a large corporation about which I had happened to write something complimentary, and how deeply satisfied I was to get a request for use of some of my material in a consumer-education class in a poverty area!

High spots? Well, as a friend of mine, also a writer, wrote to me some time ago, "Better than having a best seller is having your six-year-old take your book to school for Show and Tell!" I had always simply taken her word for it, but the day two advance copies of my first paperback juvenile arrived in the morning mail, I knew I would never forget watching Robin running happily to the afternoon school bus with one copy clutched tightly under her arm, for her Show and Tell period.

These are the fringe benefits of the writer's trade. You know how fiercely the labor unions fight for fringe benefits? Well, let me assure you that the writer's fringe benefits are worth the struggle, too. When the money you were paid is gone and you cannot even remember how much it was and what you used it for, then you may find that what sticks in your mind and pleases you most is the memory of a letter from a young girl who said that reading what you wrote was like sitting across the kitchen table from her mother and just talking.

Let's not be fatuous, imbecilic, and — well, outright dishonest? Facing the brutal facts of life, I admit I *would* trade the Board of Education's mimeographing for a $75,000 movie sale, and the letter from France for an invitation from Stockholm. I have a strong streak of impracticality, but it does have its limits. Still, I have a point to make. These fringe benefits do not depend on big sales, big successes, appearances in big magazines, publication in the tens or hundreds of thousands, and so on. They come also to writers who make small sales and have small successes — even, sometimes, to writers who manage to have nothing more published than a particularly good Letter to the Editor. In our line of work, the fringe benefits can start even before we're earning any wages at all.

It's not hard to see, either, what the common element is in most of these memorable high spots: It's the realization that you have made meaningful contact with someone, that there is actually a link between your writing and the world, yes, even between your writing and a roomful of twenty-four squirming kindergartners.

It's a nice line of work to be in — and the fringe benefits are great.

31

Where the Magic Lies

I DON'T believe in magic, and I'm not superstitious, not really. Still, I wish on stars both first and shooting, and I have a four-leaf clover crumbling to green dust in my billfold; I read my horoscope in the morning paper, and I cross my fingers when I walk up to the road where our mailbox leans under the elms, and I say, as I pull down the hatch, "Let there be something good!"

Everyone's subject to occasional lapses from rationality. Have you never knocked on wood? winced when a black cat wandered in front of you? taken an umbrella in the devout belief that it would act as insurance against precipitation? felt a little edgy after breaking a mirror? wished you didn't have to fly to Chicago on Friday the thirteenth? worn a lucky necktie or a lucky pair of socks, carried a lucky coin? And never said *Star light, star bright, first star I've seen tonight —* ? Never? Well, you win some kind of award: I think a cubical paperweight cast of solid lead would be appropriate.

I, however, sit at my desk surrounded by charms, amulets, and talismans, slogans tacked to the wall, cryptic messages to myself, and such bits of private sorcery. Once in a while I clear things away, I rearrange, I make space — but most of my symbolic objects are merely lifted, dusted under, and replaced. For the most part, I hesitate to move things; even the disorder itself becomes a sort of magical arrangement. I have been looking at two books

127

upside down in front of me for four months now, and I
haven't yet reached out to turn them right side up. I can't
tell you why, because I don't really know. Nor could I
explain most of what I have here without launching into
several lengthy and boring autobiographical anecdotes.
Why a plastic yellow-painted model of a sports car, a
Triumph TR4? Why a section of beef bone, painted red
and blue? Why an ink bottle with only a gummy residue
at the bottom? (*Not* bad housekeeping; it has survived
several dustings and sits there still.) And why, pinned to
the wall above a quotation from Emerson, a three-by-five
card with someone's initials marked on it in red ink?

There are magical acts which I perform, too, as well as
magical objects which I keep. For example, whenever
I start converting one of my messy, scratched-out, scrib-
bled-over drafts into something on white paper that an
editor can read and a printer can set type from, I always,
before I even roll Page One into the typewriter, address
the Manila envelope that will carry it on its way and prop
it up against my postal scales. And whenever I begin
rough drafts, outlines, and tentative beginnings of all
sorts, I always begin with my paper on a clipboard and
not directly on my desk — even if the clipboard is on the
desk anyway. I could go on; but let it suffice to say that
some things I do out of habit and some of my habits have
become rituals which I can no longer violate without
feeling uneasy. They have become, then, magical behavior.

I know I'm not the only one. There are writers who
have to set themselves up for each working day with a
certain number of pencils to be sharpened, a certain
passage to be read from a certain book. Others need to
wear a certain jacket, gnaw on a certain cold and unlighted
pipe.

There's no harm in all this, I suppose, as long as it

doesn't become so rigid as to incapacitate you completely if you cannot comply. If when you're out of Schlitz you're not only out of beer but out of the writing business altogether, you've got a nasty hang-up. And if your writing jacket goes to the cleaners (or worse, to the Salvation Army) and your mind goes with it, then you're in deep trouble.

But a certain amount of magic is comforting. It provides an easy and familiar framework within which to settle oneself down to business. It may also provide stimulus, motivation, a carrot in front of one's nose, a lash across one's back — all of which, for some reason or another, most writers seem to need. Why the thought of the writing itself, of its completion and of its possible publication, isn't enough, I don't know. But it isn't; not for me, anyway.

Some people are magical, too. Reminders of them can spur you on. There are friends and family for most of us, editors and fans for the fortunate; and for those who have reached the point of expecting to be remunerated, there are creditors as well.

What I need most, Emerson said, *is someone to make me do what I can.* Don't we all! I read this frequently and sigh in agreement. I can't avoid reading it frequently; it's on the wall directly in front of my nose and only two and a half feet away. I read it, and I look at the yellow Triumph and at the red-and-blue beef bone and at the three-by-five card with the magical initials on it, and I take a deep breath. "What I need most," I say to myself, and I square my shoulders and roll the paper into the typewriter, and I begin: "I don't believe in magic. . . ."

Well, it's true. I don't, not really. Because I know where the magic lies. It's not in my little yellow Triumph TR4, not in my painted bone amulet, not in the ritual of addressing the Manila envelope, not in that three-by-five card. It's not in shooting stars, not in any stars at all. The magic — like the fault, dear Brutus — is not in our stars, but in ourselves. The magic, after all, lies within.

And even though I keep that talismanic card there, that mystic beef bone, that symbolic Triumph, I know that the someone to make me do what I can has to be, in the end, *myself.*

32

All the Time in the World

I HAVE never seen anything move so fast as the hands on my clock and the pages on my calendar. I yearn for a 36-hour day, or an 8-day week, or even just a thirteenth month jammed in there somewhere, a month without appointments, without bills, without deadlines, without obligations of any kind, a month suspended between September and October or perhaps between April and May, a free month, a month for me and my thoughts and my typewriter — and no interruptions!

Time. That's what I want, time.

Oh, to have all the time in the world!

All the time in the world . . . And if I had it, how would I use it, I wonder? How would I mark it off and divide it up? How would I spend each hour, if my hours were limitless?

It will never happen. And if ever I felt, eternities ago when I was very young and days were endless and time crept and I couldn't remember last Christmas when this Christmas came — if I felt then that I truly had all the time in the world, well, I can't really remember the feeling. Nor do I remember how well I spent those endless hours, that unmarked week, those months and months — surely more than twelve? — that stretched between Christmases.

I suspect that I did not really spend them well at all.

(Time, like Youth, is wasted on the young!) But would I do much better now? I doubt it.

I have more time now than I had a number of years ago when our children were younger and more demanding. But I wrote as much then as now. In fact, I wrote more. I accomplished then in the baby's naptime what now may occupy an entire day. Did the hands of the clock move more slowly then? I don't know, but I was far too busy to watch the hands of the clock. Now, with everyone at school, I can sit at the typewriter for six or seven hours in a row if I skip my lunch — and some days I do; but for some reason I rarely complete more than a baby's-nap-time's-worth of work anyway.

"Three hours a day will produce as much as a man ought to write." That's what Anthony Trollope says, in his *Autobiography*.

More recently, Irving Petite (author of *Mr. B, The Elderberry Tree, The Best Time of Year*) has written, "I do not believe in the l-o-n-g hours that some writers . . . profess to put in." And he goes on to tell how, when he first lived on Tiger Mountain, he spent the whole day keeping his stock herded in on his fenceless property; and while he herded, the ideas gathered; and when he finally had an hour by lamplight at the end of the day, he put his ideas quickly on paper — for he was much too tired to spend any more time at it.

Last night, at the end of one of my seven-hour work-days, I was thinking of Mr. Trollope and Mr. Petite. *It's all very well for you to talk of working one hour or three hours*, I thought resentfully, *but it happens to have taken me seven, and I didn't do much at that!*

Parkinson's Law? Well, yes, it's a handy explanation: Work expands to fill the time available for its completion. But a word of Irving Petite's sticks like a burr in my mind.

Profess. . . . "the l-o-n-g hours that some writers . . . profess to put in." A question nags at me. Which meaning, in my case, should I attach to that word "profess" — affirm? practice? or *pretend?*

Had I really worked seven hours, or had I only professed to working seven hours, and had I simply wasted, utterly and disgracefully, at least four of those seven hours? Or perhaps even six of them?

For I'm sure that when Anthony Trollope and Irving Petite speak of "hours," they mean hours spent actually working — not shuffling papers, cleaning typewriter keys, glancing through the mail, examining one's cuticles, and watching the hands spin round on the clock.

All the time in the world! — It seems to me that a seven-hour stretch at the typewriter (and the possibility of another such the following day and perhaps even the day after) is, on any reasonable, human scale, pretty close to all the time in the world. And I let an awful lot of it get away from me. Why? Because, I suppose, like Mr. Petite's stock in those early days on Tiger Mountain, it hasn't much by way of fencing to keep it in.

For there are virtues in limits, after all.

When our youngest boy got his first steady job, he wrote about it in a letter home, as follows:

". . . this situation is better for me than having total freedom. . . . I mean, I think I'm realizing the value of time. When I had all the time in the world in front of me, it was easy to say, 'Well, I'm going to do something constructive tomorrow,' and then say it again the next day and again the next. But now I am face to face with a definite chunk of time and the decision of how to use it. The choice is there: to drift and dream or to make dreams come true. I don't think I've ever been confronted with this choice before, although I must have been making it all my life. I guess I just have to realize that it's up to me, and it's now or never."

There is an old Scottish proverb that tells us, "What may be done at any time will be done at no time." I have discovered that I get more writing done on a day when there are some other claims against my time — forcing me to perceive, evaluate, and decide! — than on a day when there are none whatsoever. And Anthony Trollope may be right. Three hours a day may be quite sufficient, if you come to the time and to your task ready to join the two of them tightly, leaving no slack.

No one has all the time in the world. Or perhaps every-one has it. For all the time in the world is only *now*; no one has any moment more than now that he can count upon. Your choice (and you, too, have been making it all your life) is not really between now and tomorrow; it is between now or never.

Here comes Now! Seize it, use it! — It won't come again.

33

Unpublished — Thank God

FOR the past several weeks I have been engaged in sorting, dating, annotating, and packing all the paper evidence of my literary career that I can bear to part with — pounds of correspondence with editors, publishers, and my agent; piles of manuscripts, published and unpublished, finished and unfinished; notes and jottings; carbons and galleys; fan mail; and a collection of juvenilia that has somehow survived transport from city to city, house to house, through the years.

All of this will shortly be on its way to repose in the archives of a university library, where it may lie forever untouched (in acid-free envelopes in a humidity-controlled vault, they tell me) or where it may, at some future date, provide some literary archaeologist with the bones and shards from which to reconstruct the life and hard times of an average American writer of the mid-twentieth century.

The process of going through all this material, some of which I had not even glanced at for twenty years, has been by turns invigorating, astonishing, depressing, horrifying, nostalgia-producing, and chastening. (And, I must add, a little unnerving; it bears an uneasy resemblance to making out a will, consulting an undertaker, and selecting a tombstone. I keep looking anxiously in the mirror, half-expecting to find that I've turned gray and grandmotherly overnight.)

I decided at the outset to be rigorously — disastrously, perhaps — honest. The library wanted my literary remains, albeit somewhat prematurely; they had not asked for my Selected or Favorite works. Therefore, I shall give them everything. *Everything . . .*

Sara and Michael stood at the top of the hill. The sun was like a blazing torch, and seemed to set fire to the western woods. The clouds were tinged with scarlet, and one ray of the sun — more beautiful than any of the others — struck slantingly on Sara's face and glorified her expression.

Oh, brother.

"Anything I felt that way about, *I'd* throw out," said my daughter, coming upon me in mid-groan. "I certainly wouldn't want anybody to see it."

I don't really want anybody to see it either. But once I had imagined that mythical future literary researcher grubbing away in the vaults, I could hear him. "Oh, don't throw that out!" he cries to me down the years between us. "I want to see you at your worst, too. Let me see the things you scribbled when you were young and naïve. Let me see the things you started and couldn't finish. Let me see the things nobody would buy!"

O.K., O.K. — For wouldn't it be jolly to find the contents of Chaucer's wastebasket? the drafts that Virgil discarded? the puerile beginnings of Shakespeare's skill? the doggerel Dante scratched away at when he was just a boy?

Well, I'm only sorry my talent is not the equal of theirs, so that my abortive efforts and juvenilia would prove of equivalent interest. Nevertheless, it shall be preserved, from my funeral verse to a broken chinaware elephant toothbrush-holder through imitation Sandburg, imitation

Walpole, imitation stories for imitation Shirley Temple movies, embarrassing romances, ghastly librettos for comic operettas, humorous essays to make their author weep three decades later, and innumerable grim tragedies full of sudden blindness, disfiguring scars, madness, suicide, amnesia, murder; yes, I shall even send along a poem beginning, *The jungle palms waved lazily,/The moon was full and bright;/The silence brooded over all/In the middle of the night./The jungle creatures forth did creep,/Their prey to stalk and kill* . . . (Good grief! The jungle creatures FORTH DID CREEP?!)

I sat at the kitchen table last night and shriveled while my daughter-in-law leafed through the whole mortifying mess. She turned the pages silently, doggedly, to the end. For some reason or other, I could rather blithely ship it off to a library, but to see her reading it, actually *reading* it, turned me as pink as my poor lamented elephant. . . . *Pinky was an elephant/(The pieces — there were seven)/Pinky was an elephant,/But his soul has gone to heaven.* (The first time I ever turned a personal tragedy into art! My first pearl, produced from a painful grit! — I was ten, so forgive me.)

The inescapable question, it seemed to me, was, How could anyone have seen one iota of talent in all that unutterable garbage? — My teachers saw talent. And if they were right, what remarkable vision! How did they do it?

"The thing is," my daughter-in-law asked, *"how much was anybody else writing?"*

Of course. A major symptom of talent (whether it be said *I* have any or not) must be just sheer quantity. For quantity is necessary. Quantity there must be, if quality is to be achieved. The cream of your work has to have something to float on, something to rise to the top of; and this applies, I think, even after the boundaries of the juvenile are passed. I have been sorting, dating, annotating, and packing all *that,* too: the dozens of post-juvenile scripts which have been languishing unfinished and/or unpublished in my files for years.

It is a salutary experience to sit me down and come to a series of quick decisions about these scripts. Anything with more than a shred of hope to it, I am keeping — at least until the next shipment; all the rest, off, off, begone! I know I'll never finish this novel about incest and infanticide and murder and madness, or this science fiction story, outrun by fact; no one will ever produce this terrible television play — and come to think of it, I'm glad no one ever did. So, as I drop the scripts into a sturdy carton, my only bow to censorship is to annotate here and there, along with the information "Unpublished," an additional "Thank God!"

34

The Ten Percent Fantasy Figure

YOUNG girls may be too cool these days to dream of the perfect and handsome prince, and upper-middle-class housewives may be too disillusioned to dream of the perfect maid or even of the perfect cleaning lady; but most writers still dream, now and then, of the perfect literary agent.

The agent is a central fantasy figure in the writer's daydream of success. The non-selling writer is certain that if he had an agent, he would sell. The selling writer is certain that if he had the right agent, the perfect agent, he'd sell more — and at higher prices. Off in the distance, standing on the horizon, the perfect agent glimmers and beckons. Behind him, its gates ready to swing open at his touch, the Golden City of Success rises with its spires glowing and its pennants fluttering, pennants that look remarkably like five-figure checks and publishers' contracts.

"Take me to your leader!" becomes, in the mouth and from the pen of the beginning writer, "Lead me to your agent!" And the writer who has an agent (like me, for example) growls and grumbles and mutters evasively. Or, perhaps, snaps back with the sting of truth: Are you sure you need one?

How many scripts do you have making the rounds? How much have you sold on your own? If you have to hem and haw when you answer those questions, you're not ready for an agent. For you don't *need* an agent until, in a sense, *you don't need an agent*. The hinge of the paradox is that you don't need an agent until he needs — or wants — you. When you look like money to him, then he'll be glad to try to get it and share it with you. And he shares it in a generous split — 90% for you, 10% for him.

The inequity of that division is something to ponder. Calculate, if you will, how many writers of your earning capacity an agent would have to handle in order to live one cut above poverty level in New York City. That's not an enjoyable calculation, at least not for me. There have been years when 10% of my earnings couldn't have provided for my agent's cat; and even my best years have probably done no more than to give him one month's bare subsistence out of the twelve. It's a sobering thought.

There are agents who will handle you if you haven't sold — for a fee, a reading fee, payable in advance. Do you want my advice on this matter? Here it is: *Don't do it*. Agents who are really agents make their income from selling manuscripts, *not from reading them*. Your manuscript belongs in the hands of a man who can't make a penny from it until he's sold it to someone else, not in the hands of a man who has your five-, ten-, or twenty-five dollar check before he even starts to think about what he might do with your work — if, indeed, he ever thinks about it at all. Only the genuine agent, working for ten percent of sales, has a real stake in *your* success.

Of course, you don't have to have an agent, you know. You've heard it before, from me, from others: no agent can sell the unsalable. Any script an agent can sell, you can sell.

Then why have an agent? Why do *I* have an agent? Because I'd rather write than sell, that's why, and the time he spends selling what I write, *I* can spend writing more of it.

Here's what a good agent can do for you. He can save you the work of constant submission and resubmission of scripts; and he can save you the agony of seeing every rejection. He can get you the foreign sales and the secondary rights and the out-of-the-way acceptances you might not even know where to look for. He can speed things up. He can mention you over lunch with Mr. Editor. He can find out, while the waiter pours the coffee, what some particular magazine is really hankering for — and he can remember that you have it, or can do it. He can keep his eye on the market while you keep yours on the typewriter.

A good agent is a good bargainer (which good writers are often *not*) — and when a good agent submits your script, his good reputation backs it up.

I've had the same agent for over twenty years. And no, I won't lead you to him — ! Twenty years is a long time, and we're not tied to each other with any contract or agreement on paper. The basis of our relationship is simply the trust each of us has that the other is doing his best. Somebody once asked me how I knew I was getting all the money that was actually coming to me. I could only say that I hadn't any way of *knowing,* but that the minute I thought I wasn't, it'd be all over between us. Once mistrust enters, the agent-writer relationship, like a doctor-patient relationship, blows sky-high and had best be terminated, on the spot.

What has my agent done for me? In the first place, he's more than earned his ten percent of all I've made in those twenty years; far from begrudging him any of it, I am pained to consider how hard he has had to work for so little. He's sold scripts to markets I didn't know existed. He's resurrected old stories and sent me checks for them years after I'd forgotten I'd ever written them. He's needled me now and then when I've required needling. More often, he's cheered me up. He's never forgotten me at Christmas — and I remember fondly how he advanced me some money at a time when I wasn't making enough for his ten percent commission to keep him in cigarettes.

Is he the perfect agent?

No, he isn't. The perfect agent is a magician who casts spells over editors and publishers, causing them to suspend their critical faculties when confronted with your scripts. The perfect agent is an alchemist who turns the lead of a dud script into gold and sends you a check for the proceeds. The perfect agent is a literary wizard who can tell you what five words to change in your latest story to make it sound as if it were written by Ray Bradbury or Isaac Bashevis Singer.

The perfect agent stands resplendent on the horizon — and like the horizon itself, he forever recedes as you approach. Forget him. Concentrate, instead, upon the perfect script.

A few perfect — or almost-perfect — scripts, and you'll be able to find your agent. Not perfect. But *good*.

35

Goats, Moors, and Harley Street

WHEN I was a little girl, one of my favorite books was Johanna Spyri's *Heidi*. It wasn't Heidi herself so much that I loved, or the story; it was the bed in the hayloft of Grandfather's hut, and the bread and the cheese and the milk, and above all else, the goats. Oh, the goats! I thought of them again when I watched *Heidi* on television some time ago and found myself weeping. For I wasn't shedding tears about Heidi or Klara or Peter or Grandfather — I was being sentimental about (1) myself when young, and (2) those goats.

I remember once coming upon a herd of goats high in an alpine pasture in the Rockies. If I could have had my wish, I would have settled down right then and there to herd them, and who knows, I might be there yet. And I remember, too, that when we first came to live in this house, one of the neighbor-children came to get acquainted, and tagging along behind her was her pet goat, a tiny black kid with white markings. What a darling it was, so tender and sweet and delicate that I dropped to my knees to embrace it — and felt my eyes, once more, filling up with tears.

It all goes back to *Heidi*, of course. I'm not sure I'd ever seen a goat when I first read *Heidi*. Maybe at the zoo — but I suspect that I didn't really *notice* goats until after I read *Heidi* or had it read to me. Then, when I did notice goats, I was prepared to love them; and I've loved them immoderately ever since.

So it's all Miss Spyri's fault. Because of her I have always wanted, in my secret heart, to live in a hut and have goats to herd, and make my meals of bread and cheese and milk, and sleep in a hayloft with a hole in the rafters to look out from. Because of her, I cry over goats.

So much for goats. What did I say next? — Moors. Well, *I never saw a moor, / I never saw the sea; / Yet know I how the heather looks, / And what a wave must be.* That's Emily Dickinson, and like her, I've never seen a moor either, not yet. But I've read *The Secret Garden* by Frances Hodgson Burnett over and over, as a child myself and to my own children, countless times; and there is a moor swept with a fresh spring wind, as favorite a place to me as any real place I've been. (Or maybe I should say, as *real* a place to me as any favorite place I've been — !) And if ever I travel to Yorkshire and walk out upon the moor, I'll be prepared, it won't seem strange, and I know the splendid joy of recognition that I'll feel . . .

For we were in London one summer, my husband and I. And early one evening we went for a long, aimless walk, going nowhere in particular and not even knowing exactly where we were. London had already far outrun my expectations; I found I needed only to step upon its sidewalks and the London I had secreted away from a hundred novels, the London of my English literary heritage (which I really didn't know I had until that moment) suddenly sprang into life. A little blue and white sign on a building told me, "Edward Lear lived here." — Oh, Owl, Oh, Pussy-cat! — and beneath my feet in Westminster Abbey there was a name on the worn stone: *Geoffrey Chaucer*. And on that evening, walking along, a lavender evening, soft and mild, no one about, the street deserted

— I took a breath and stopped short. What was it? Something in the air, the scent of — of — ether? chloroform? iodoform? *Doctors' offices,* I thought, and then, *Harley Street!* Harley Street, where else could I be but on Harley Street, where in a half-dozen novels London doctors had taken up their practices? "It's Harley Street!" I said out loud, and at the corner the signs proved me right.

I don't really remember in what books I first met Harley Street, but this morning in the public library I took a copy of Maugham's *Of Human Bondage* from the shelf, and thumbed it until I found, on page 294, the phrase, "take a consulting-room in Harley Street . . . and . . . become prosperous, eminent, and titled," so there at least was one place. But I've never forgotten that moment when that unmistakable Aesculapian smell brought the world of my books and the grey stones of a London street together into one.

What I am trying to say — with the goats and the moors and Harley Street — is that reading is not apart from life, a retreat, an escape, but on the contrary creates a rich network of meanings, feelings, associations, and attitudes that subtly form, color, and transform our reactions to the "realities" we meet in life. The more and more deeply we read, the more intricately connected and rooted are these things. It is not merely a matter of being able to make or to recognize a literary allusion; it's much more than that. Objects and experiences are infused from literature with more than their present and momentary meaning as we meet them. Some of this wealth of association is public, general, and expectable. What is a balcony, for example? — A platform that juts out from the wall of a building, is enclosed by a railing, and is accessible by entrance from within. But how long can you (or almost anyone) think about a balcony without thinking of Romeo and Juliet? And it would be easy to come up with a dozen such examples in the next dozen minutes. But there is also in each of us a private hoard of such associations, and much of it I suppose we could not even identify or track to its ultimate sources, though it's fun to try. Still, it's there, even if we can't always locate it on page 294.

I often think that it must be a most wonderful thing to write words that forever form or change someone's view of goats, or of God, of lilacs, or of love; and I am pleased now and then to realize that in a very small way I have done something like that, or at least so I have been told — for through me a lot of people seem to have stumbled upon a singular perception, a fact which they had never before comprehended: that writers are indeed *human*. If I accomplish nothing else, I *have* done that.

But isn't this what we all do? For if you have written and published, then you too have added shading and nuance to someone's perception of something — or of many things, perhaps. You may not ever create an unforgettable character, or add a word to the language, or make millions of people think of you when they see a balcony; but whatever you write does not remain black-on-white, mere printer's ink upon the page, ultimately to fade and crumble. It moves instead into the mind and heart of your reader, and there it takes up residence, to play its part in how he sees the world — goats, moors, Harley Street, and all.

36

Vanity by Any Other Name

I ADMIT that it's a tough business. It takes a lot of sweat in the first place simply to write a book. And then it takes courage to send it out, patience to wait, and fortitude to endure its return; and courage again to send it out again, and more patience to wait some more, and fortitude beyond measure, over and over and over. No wonder an occasional writer is gripped by the urge to bypass the whole ordeal. It's perfectly understandable.

You've written a book. You want it published. You want to pick it up and hold it in your hand, solid, between covers, dust-jacketed, with your name on it: your book. Those are compelling words, *your book.* The faster you can get from your manuscript to Your Book, the better — right?

I have a brochure here on my desk. It says YOUR BOOK right on its cover. It says a lot of other things inside. For example, it says:

> As many important and famous writers of the past have done, you can turn to investment publishing.
>
> Many prominent writers have invested in their own works because, if they had not, success might have eluded them.
>
> Edgar Allan Poe published his first book, *Tamerlane,* anonymously at his own expense.
>
> Henry David Thoreau's first work, *A Week on the Con-*

cord and Merrimack Rivers, was published at his own expense.

And so on. So why not you?

The brochure I have here on my desk talks about "investment publishing." Elsewhere you will hear the terms "subsidy publishing" or "cooperative publishing." But when professional writers, editors, book reviewers, critics, and the operators of bookstores are talking, the word you hear will not be investment, or cooperative, or subsidy; it will be *vanity.* And the basic reality is this: the vanity publisher is like the literary agent who charges a reading fee, while the royalty publisher, on the other hand, is like the agent who takes only a ten percent commission from sales. The vanity publisher takes your money along with your manuscript, and attempts to keep his printing costs below your investment, in order to turn a profit even if no books sell. The royalty publisher pays all the costs of publishing and, like the genuine agent, cannot make a profit unless he manages to sell your book.

The vanity publisher may, indeed, try to sell your book. But he is operating under a number of handicaps. First, if he's kept your investment within reasonable bounds, he isn't going to have much to spend on promotion. Second, most booksellers do not welcome vanity press publications with open arms and do not stock them in quantity. Third, it is almost impossible for a vanity press book to achieve notice in the magazines and newspapers where books are reviewed. "We make every effort to obtain reviews in prominent periodicals," says the brochure on my desk. Perhaps so — but I also have on my desk a clipping from The Seattle *Times,* with this sentence marked: "The Times book editor, as a matter of general policy, does not review books published by vanity-press houses." It is possible that such a policy may consign a few worthwhile books to silence, but it is an understandable policy; for the most part, vanity publications are of little or no literary merit or potential readership.

Who resorts to the vanity publishers, and why? Is vanity itself the prime motivation? the only motivation? As a matter of fact, in some cases the business might be called, variously, naïveté press, or paranoid publishing, or thin-skinned editions, or perhaps impatient imprints. There are those who turn to the vanity publishers because they have been rejected beyond endurance (for them, desperation houses?) — and there are those who have been rejected a few times and have decided, perhaps prematurely, to try no more. Some have not even tried at all to win acceptance from a royalty publishing house; perhaps (a) they believe it is impossible without pull or connections, or (b) they have seen the vanity publisher's advertisements and are too uninformed to know the difference, or (c) they are afraid of being rejected and would rather not place themselves in that peril. Some of the last may even believe that they will some day be recognized for the geniuses they are — but for now, they'd rather not be told otherwise. No vanity publisher will tell them otherwise.

And what happens to these people? Once in a very great while somebody comes up a winner. But the usual story is more like that of the woman who paid $1600 to have her book of poems published — and has so far received ten dollars and eighty cents in return. It seems to me that in order not to be seriously damaged by such an experience, the vanity press writer must be so delighted by the mere physical existence of the books themselves that he doesn't care about anything else. As for vanity, as long as you pay instead of *being paid,* your vanity (and we all have it, in some measure) will never be truly assuaged.

Is there ever any good and valid reason for paying for

the publication of your own books? Well, if you have
written a family history, or something of very local appeal,
or an account of the growth of the Acme Tuning-Fork
Company to be given to your tuned-in customers, you are
not likely to interest Knopf or David McKay or Grove
Press; in which case, what do you do? Go to a printer. A
local printer can probably do the job for you at a reasonable price, and once you have the books in hand you can
sell them (perhaps with the aid of a jobber) or give them
away, as best you can, without having been seduced by any
promises or fed any daydreams over which to break your
heart.

What about Poe and Thoreau, who "invested in their
own works because, if they had not, success might have
eluded them"?

Let's see. Poe published *Tamerlane* in 1827. Then he
struggled along for eight years virtually unnoticed, finally
joined the staff of the *Southern Literary Messenger* and
was able, as a staff writer, to earn something from his
writing. It wasn't until the 1840's that he really came into
the public eye. People *did* take note of *The Raven*, which
was published in 1845. Four years later Poe was dead.
What good it did him to pay for the publication of *Tamerlane* — not even under his own name, but just by "A
Bostonian" — I don't know.

As for Thoreau, well, let me tell you. Henry David
Thoreau published two books during his lifetime. *A Week
on the Concord and Merrimack Rivers* came out in 1849.
One thousand copies were printed. Four years later, the
printer shipped the 706 copies remaining to Concord, and
poor Henry lugged them up to his folks' attic and then
wrote in his journal, "I have now a library of nearly nine
hundred volumes, over seven hundred of which I wrote
myself." He had optimistically announced, with the print-

ing of *A Week* etc., "soon to be published: *Walden,*" but *soon* (after the dull thud of his privately financed venture) stretched into five years. And when *Walden* finally *was* published, nobody took much notice of it; I suspect that Henry turned not much more profit on it than he did on the celebrated bean-field whose outgo and income he calculates to the halfpenny in the book's seventh chapter — eight dollars, seventy-one and one-half cents.

Of course Thoreau did become famous (though not rich) some time after his death; which is better than not becoming famous at all — but still is not much recommendation for "investment publishing." Clearly, despite their investments, success eluded both Poe and Thoreau. And the portion of their posthumous fame that can be laid to their having paid for their own first publication is, by generous estimate, a few thousandths of a decimal point this side of *nil.*

Please — *don't!*

37

A Note from My Real Office

OUR middle daughter went recently with a group of classmates to visit the state capital. When she returned, she reported that they had all met with the Governor in his office.

"Well, that is, in the office where he meets people," Jill amended, "not in his *real* office. I mean, I'm sure he has a real office where he works, *and that wasn't it.*"

The basis for Jill's judgment in this matter is perfectly clear to me. Today, when in one of my periodic seizures of housewifery I decided to clean Jill's room and swept everything into a big heap for her to sort out when she gets back from school, I thought, Well, this is Jill's real room, there's no doubt about it. And as I Scotch-taped a threatening note to her door (signed MOM THE TERRIBLE, with skull and crossbones), I remembered the disturbing business of Henry Miller's studio, which has been bothering me for a number of months.

The frontispiece to *The Books in My Life* by Henry Miller is a photograph which purports to show Henry Miller in his studio, sitting at his desk. Now, I have always imagined Henry Miller at work in a leaf-pile of papers, surrounded by ends of garlic sausage, rinds of cheese, half-drunk mugs and glasses of various beverages, overflowing ashtrays, and heels of stale French bread. But in this photograph there he sits, at a desk as pristine and neat as the

desk of a corporation executive who has just been kicked
upstairs to become a highly paid man-of-no-work. The
studio behind and around him is alarmingly tidy. There
is something almost antiseptic about it. When I look at
the photograph, I smell furniture polish. Henry, something in me cries out, surely you don't write in that studio?
Henry, where is your *real* studio?

Here at my real desk in my real office, which is half of
a very large real bedroom, I let my eye wander over a cold
cup of yesterday's coffee, a shuffle of bills and unanswered
mail, a Pisa-tower of books topped with a box of raisins,
a business card from an antique shop, two bottles of glue,
and — well — a number of other things. There is at any
rate no redolence of furniture polish here; one would be
hard put to find a five-inch square of desk surface to use
it on.

I know! — Someone in the Henry Miller ménage, appre-
hensive of the approaching trauma of a formal photograph,
must have called in a cleaning lady to straighten things
up. That's it. *She's* been there, without a doubt, one of
those "domestics who do, indeed, tidy our writing tables
and ruthlessly make an end of all disorder, but, by their
consistent and systematic methods, sweep away or destroy,
stupidly and senselessly, the fruits of years of laborious
work."

That quote about cleaning ladies is from Theodor Reik,
the psychoanalyst, speaking in his classic work, *Listening
with the Third Ear*. What better and more authoritative-
sounding defense of slovenliness could you ask for?

Well, I've tried being neat and orderly, but it just
doesn't work. At least it doesn't work for very long. As
the pace of my labor increases, the mess about me increases; that's ordinary and expectable enough. But somewhere along the way a reciprocal process begins to show

itself. As the mess increases, so the pace increases, and not only the pace, but the amount of inventiveness, the quality of the work itself. The very act of gazing idly at my rubble-heaped desk, or of rummaging through it all in search of this or that, seems to provoke thought and engender ideas. I might even go so far as to paraphrase Robert Herrick and say, "A sweet disorder on my desk/Kindles in me creativeness," which is not much of a rhyme but is a pretty thought, and true.

It's my experience that orderliness, while admirable in many respects, can simply be carried too far. For one thing, it can waste a tremendous amount of time; if you are constantly tidying up after yourself, or constantly setting up your work and making elaborate preparations for it, how much time are you consuming that could be spent actually getting the work *done*? (Answer: quite a lot.) But for another thing, extreme orderliness can act subtly to inhibit creativity. It draws boundaries between areas of thought, and keeps ideas and facts from sloshing over and reacting one with another. It does away with chance juxtapositions and cross-fertilization. And it works constantly against the happy occurrences of serendipity.

For if you always have "a place for everything, and everything in its place," as recommended by Samuel Smiles, the *Self-Help* man, how are you ever going to discover anything by glorious accident? Do you remember what Robert Crichton (*The Secret of Santa Vittoria*) said about his shoe-box full of sloppy and haphazard notes? — "my compost pile, a dung heap for potential fertility," he called it. Samuel Smiles would be shaking his head and tsk-tsk-ing; but, turning to an essayist of a higher order, I am pleased to find Montaigne saying, "There is no course of life so weak and sottish as that which is managed by order, method, and discipline." That bucks me up considerably, especially when I have to sort through all the crumpled-up, rough-draft pages in my wastebasket in order to find the paper I was calculating my revised estimated tax on. . . .

I read in an article somewhere that one reason children are not often very creative in school is that they are con·tinuously under pressure to clean up and put things away. Every schoolroom project is interrupted innumerable times for the ruthless domesticity required by the pedagogical cleaning ladies whose patron saint is probably Samuel Smiles himself. Who, the writer of the article wanted to know, *who* can be truly creative under such hampering circumstances? (I don't recall where I read that. I think there's a note on it somewhere, but finding it in all this mess is an unlikely prospect and I'm not going to waste time looking. Take my word for it. I read it — somewhere.)

Our daughters are all fairly creative; as for mess, however, the two younger ones are unsurpassed. Jill, on being told to clean up her room, will say peevishly, "What's wrong with it?" But Robin, with that genius for phrases of the very young, responded recently to the same request with an outraged howl: "But this is the only way a little kid can live!"

If you are by nature orderly and neat, and it comes easily to you, taking up no extra time and effort, I won't try to change you. I am simply soothing the consciences of the rest of us, for we suffer recurrent pangs of guilt — brainwashed by mothers and schoolteachers and devoted followers of Samuel Smiles — and need to be reminded that Creation has always come out of Chaos, even in the Beginning, and that the prizes and surprises of serendipitous discoveries are unlikely to happen in a thoroughly domesticated, pigeon-holed, alphabetized world where all is exactly where you expect to find it.

This is the only way a little kid, a noted psychoanalyst, and a best-selling novelist can live. It works best for me, too.

I hope Henry Miller didn't lose the fruits of too many years of laborious work, just to have that picture taken!

38

Portrait of the Artist As an Oyster

HAPPINESS is, we all know, a warm letter from the editor, with check enclosed. Happiness is your name on the cover, and a dust-jacket photograph that makes you look both attractive and intelligent. Happiness is a Library of Congress number. Happiness is a favorable review in *The New York Times*. Happiness is a stack of fan mail. Happiness is a Pulitzer Prize.

If you could just *be* a writer, a reasonably successful writer, you'd be happy, wouldn't you?

Sure.

Well — "Authorship," says Erskine Caldwell in his *Writing in America,* "is not a profession that either creates or tolerates happiness in a human being."

That seems to be about as unequivocal a statement as you could ask for on the subject of writers and happiness. Do you suppose the man could be right?

And what about the assertions of the infamous (in literary circles) Dr. Edmund Bergler, author of *The Writer and Psychoanalysis,* who sees the writer as a neurotic personality, depressed, fearful, unhappy, and about as normal as a two-headed calf? Normal people just don't write, writes Dr. Bergler. (Of course he may be using *not writing* as one of the criteria for "normal," while, conversely and circularly, *writing* automatically puts you in the "not normal" category.)

157

I hate to agree with Dr. Bergler in the least, and for the most part I don't; but there is a core of truth there. As William Styron has said, "The good writing of any age has always been the product of *somebody's* neurosis, and we'd have a mighty dull literature if all the writers that came along were a bunch of happy chuckleheads." Note, incidentally, how Styron puts down happiness with that "bunch of happy chuckleheads" bit. Happiness is just a hair's breadth this side of imbecility, and if it escapes being altogether sterile, it's likely to breed something "mighty dull."

It is true, isn't it? Writers brood too much and are too sensitive. Writers tend to be shy and tense. Writers are gloomy and manic by fits and starts. Writers spend a lot of time examining life — others' lives and their own as well — and if the unexamined life is not worth living, the examined life always proves to have ghastly flaws. Writers drink too much, smoke too much. Writers earn erratically, spend erratically, and worry. Writers make their families miserable and are made miserable in return. Of course, none of these things is peculiar to writers, and not all writers fit the list in all particulars; but, taken as a group, writers tend to exhibit these items of behavior in more extreme forms than — shall we say? — normal people, i.e. non-writers.

What about me? Oh, I'm not an alcoholic, nor am I any kind of smoker from chain on down, but otherwise I'll take the fifth. I will admit, however, that I am not at the present time, nor have I ever been, a happy chucklehead. (This fact does not in itself make me a good writer, of course. I'm not even sure that it preserves me from being dull. I've always had the impression that I had to work a little at not being dull; if not being dull were just a function of being miserable, how gloriously easy it would be to be unfailingly fascinating!) But even if I'm not a happy chucklehead, surely I am, for the most part, happy? Well, yes, I'm happy; I'm happy now and I'm happy then, and I'm also unhappy now and then. And I'm both happy and unhappy from causes both within and without my writing, and often the within and the without are so tangled and inextricably snarled together that they make the Gordian knot look like a granny.

As far as writing is concerned, if happiness comes from being loved, I tend to feel loved only until the glow from a successful piece of writing fades (a rapid process!). Or, if happiness is to do your own true work — Marcus Aurelius' definition — well, I am usually convinced, between bouts of work, that I have lost the ability to do it altogether, and I consequently wallow in misery until by some miracle I am at it again. So it is, I think, that among writers, happy chuckleheads are few.

But we who write are blessed as is the oyster, for we, too, can work a transformation upon our sufferings, both great and small. We can with our minor irritations provoke laughter, and with our major griefs and sorrows move others to tears, to understanding, to self-recognition. I think of William Gibson's beautiful cry of anguish, *A Mass for the Dead,* and I think of Anne Sexton's poetry; and I believe that there is in this gift, this singular gift for transfiguration, a peculiar joy and exaltation beyond mere happiness. But I think also of the inside pages of my morning newspaper, and of the sweetness of laughter that turns my headline-soured coffee back into something drinkable. For that cheerful benison I thank you, Art Buchwald, Russell Baker: Yours is the same singular gift in another (much-needed!) manifestation.

And I think, finally, of some few things of my own — few, yes, because of course not everything is the product

of such transfiguration — of several short stories, a handful of poems, and I remember the incalculable satisfaction
I felt when I had finished them, even though whatever
had grieved me was still there. For in the engrossing, difficult process of art, the artist is healed, comforted, and
eased (even as is the oyster), and in some sense may be
transformed himself by the act of working a transformation upon life.

I read somewhere that a pearl is the product of "a sick
oyster." I don't know about the word "sick" — *bothered*
would be better, perhaps, or *irritated*. Anyway, maybe a
malacologist would agree with me if I were to say, "Normal oysters just don't make pearls." O.K., then, *normal
people* (i.e. happy chuckleheads?) *don't write.*

"The only way to be happy," Flaubert says, "is to shut
yourself up in art, and count everything else as nothing."
Well, I don't know the only way to be happy, if there is
an only way (which I doubt), but I wonder: How could
an oyster make a pearl if there were nothing inside his
tightly-shut shell to trouble him?

Art is not something to shut yourself up in, while
counting everything else as nothing. It is instead an al-
chemy, a metamorphosis, for which everything else provides you with your materials. Happiness is learning how.

39

Lamb, Onions, God, and All

SOME pages back, I recommended a cookbook to you: *A Cookbook for Poor Poets and Others,* by Ann Rogers. It might well be, I suggested, a basic volume in any writer's library, along with dictionary, thesaurus, Fowler, and Bartlett. It's basic in mine, anyway. In fact, I have a loaf of Yeast Bread for Busy Poets in the oven right now, even though these lines with which I am busy are not particularly poetic. It's a fine book, cookable (try her chicken fricassee with white wine and gin, page 117) and also readable.

Not all cookbooks try to be readable, of course, but some do make an attempt at it, with little prefatory notes from contributing cooks who are usually Metropolitan opera stars or prima ballerinas, or the author's old Ukrainian grandmother, or Danny Kaye. Some succeed in a modest way; others plod drearily through sift and cream, beat and simmer, chill and serve, through soups, salads, meats, casseroles, and so on, to the sweet and surfeiting end, winding up with a section on "Cooking with a French Accent" or "How to Serve Wines." You can't read a cookbook like that; you can hunt through it, and you can follow a recipe in it, but you can't sit down and *read* it.

The other day, however, I ran across what must be one of the most readable cookbooks of all time: *The Supper of the Lamb,* by Robert Farrar Capon.

161

I must have read a review or some mention of it some weeks or months before, because I had it on the list in my billfold, my list of books I've been meaning to read or hoping to buy, books to look for in second-hand bookstores, books I'm waiting for the library to finish cataloging, books to remember when affluence strikes — or if not affluence, at least self-indulgence. Anyway, there it was on my list and there it was on the shelf. I took it home.

The Supper of the Lamb is a cookbook like no other. It is a cookbook written by an Episcopal priest, and it contains about eighty pages of recipes. But for the most part it is concerned with one long, four-part recipe which, with digressions, occupies about seventy per cent of the book. The digressions? — ah, the digressions! — well, no, they're not really digressions, come to think of it. But whatever they are — prayers, exhortations, meditations, anathemas, graces, and an eight-page essay on an onion — they are wonderful.

Although I fell in love with Father Capon almost immediately, I don't guarantee that you will. You may disagree with him violently. Or, since this is a cookbook, perhaps I should say that he may disagree with you. You may bridle at being ordered about; you may find his opinions insufferable — and he is full of opinions. But I defy you to read the first nine pages of *The Supper of the Lamb* and not acknowledge that you have met a real, live, breathing, human being. A person. A man. *Somebody.*

What first endeared him to me was simply the way he begins. Which is — simply. Page one of *The Supper of the Lamb* is headed "Ingredients," and starts off, "Let me begin without ceremony." Whereupon we launch immediately into the recipe — or into the ingredients, at least — for "Lamb for Eight Persons Four Times." And then, having finished with the list of ingredients by page three, we pick up a knife — and then we put it down again, because we aren't going to get any farther than the ingredients until we hit page twenty-nine, where we start peeling onions, smashing garlic, and scraping carrots. Clearly, this is no book for anyone in a hurry. If your thoughts on cookery run to Magic Fifteen-Minute Meals put together out of cans and little plastic packets, you don't have time to read Father Capon's recipe, much less to cook it.

As I said, the beginning of the book endeared him to me. And also his confession at the end of his list of ingredients on page three: "I am an author who had always intended to write about cooking, but who had never gotten started in a way that didn't carry him out of the field in two paragraphs or less. This time, as you can see, I have outwitted the muse." Then, of course, come the twenty-six pages of interruption. . . .

What does he interrupt himself for? — An essay on peeling an onion, a lecture on knives, an anecdote about fried parsley, a prayer.

And what does all this have to do with writing?

Suppose, I thought (after finishing the book and giving it a sort of hug), suppose this book hadn't been written yet. Suppose we wrote up a prospectus for it, a proposal, a kind of grant application. We would describe it thus: a book on cooking (more or less), with one basic recipe (sort of) running through the whole thing, but with essays and prayers and maledictions and all manner of what-not thrown in as it goes along, so that it takes nearly two hundred pages to get from one end of the recipe to the other; the whole to be written by an Episcopalian priest, a Professor of Dogmatic Theology who teaches Greek, has a beard and six children, plays the recorder, disdains Teflon but loves canned ravioli, keeps as a sort of pet a bottle of a terrible synthetic kirsch made by an insecticide company, is called by his children the walking garbage pail, and talks of God in the middle of talking of shredded cabbage.

A cookbook with prayers in it? And bits of Latin? And twenty-six pages between the ingredients of a recipe and any notion of what to do with them? And a citation addressed to bicarbonate of soda as Most Extraordinary Ordinary Thing in the World: "Friend of the flatulent, Soother of the savage, scotch-soaked breast, and blessed Bestower of peaceful sleep after four beers, two heroes, and a sausage pizza . . ."?

The grants-in-aid committee of the Truffle Foundation for the Support of Cookbook Writing deeply regrets —

There are, in fact, times when I seriously doubt that one should submit an unwritten book even to a committee composed of one's own second thoughts. We all have such committees, and they probably have their true and proper functions. But the prejudging and damnation of unwritten work is not one of them. Second thoughts second, please. Writing should come first.

I've been thinking of writing a cookbook.

But you're not a cook, you're a priest. Why not write about that?

What do you mean, "that"?

Oh, religion, God, you know — *that*.

Well, I thought I might throw some of *that* in.

Into a cookbook? You must be mad. A cookbook is made up of recipes.

Well, yes —

You *were* intending to put recipes in it?

Well, some recipes. Mainly, I —

Mainly you what?

Mainly I thought I'd just tell how to cook a leg of lamb.

Just *a leg of lamb?*

Well, sort of. I'd throw in some other things, but mostly the leg of lamb.

Not everybody likes lamb.
I didn't figure everybody would like my book, either.
Then why write it, you fathead?

Fortunately, either there was no such confrontation, or else Father Capon just didn't listen. He went ahead, began without ceremony, threw everything into the pot — lamb, onions, God, and all — and the result is a book that not everybody will like but that some people will like inordinately. I, for one; and I am glad Father Capon didn't submit it to some ultra-sensible committee (whether inner or outer) when it was just an idea in his head.

My files are full of scripts finished but unpublished, things that didn't make the grade. But what I really regret are some of my unwritten scripts, the non-products of times when I failed to follow my first heady fancies but listened instead to the dour and negative pronouncements of my second-thoughts committee, meeting untimely and ahead of schedule. And once denied, that first enthusiasm is hard to rekindle.

I haven't yet cooked a leg of lamb according to Father Capon's directions, but I recommend to you his (implicit) recipe for writing a book. Just begin without ceremony, do it your own way, and let it be you.

What else can I say? My bread is done; it smells — poetic.

40

Tellers and Sellers of Dreams

THERE are mornings of doubt.

I rise early, a handful of minutes before the sun. As I prod the thermostat upward with my forefinger and fill the kettle at the kitchen sink, the last street lights go out, blink, blink, blink. Still in my robe and pajamas, I go crunching across the frost-spiked grass to get the morning paper. By the time coffee is poured and the children wakened, I know that there are riots here and guerrilla warfare there, and the pop of the toaster reminds me that thousands, no, *millions* of people on this earth would regard my scanty breakfast (the toast is not for me, only unsugared coffee and a glass of juice) as a feast. I turn a page. "Mom?" I look up. "Would you pass me the milk, please?" Somewhere, as I put down my cup, some other mother is watching her children starve.

But my husband and the children leave for campus and school, and I shove dirty clothes and dirty dishes into their respective machines and settle down to my share of the world's work — writing fiction.

There is in most people a little suspicion of the writer, possibly even a downright conviction that he is, if not a no-good character, at least a parasite on the economic body. Along with occasional awe (*You make these things up out*

166

of your own head?) there is also an incredulity which manages slyly to imply lack of merit and undeserved reward
(*You mean you get paid that much for just TWO pages?*).
And not only ignorant, semiliterate folk feel this way;
there are many writers, some distinguished ones among
them, who hurry to dismiss themselves as "mere en-
tertainers" and their product as ephemeral and trivial.
Some claim in dust-jacket blurbs to have become writers
because they failed at everything else they tried (append-
ing, usually, long and humorous lists of failed occupations), which, of course, may be true, for a lot of people
try several wrong careers before finding the right one.
Still, you rarely hear a doctor admit — or *brag?* — that
he couldn't make the grade as a trombone player or a city
refuse collector and wound up, much to his astonishment,
in medical school. We are all, even writers, infected with
the endemic distrust mankind has for the man who writes.

So on a morning when starvation, misery, and death
flavor my orange juice, it is inescapable for me to wonder
why I am not building houses, feeding the hungry, creating part of the world's wealth, producing its crops, doing
something that matters.

But when this overcomes me, I look back, not over my
own life, but down the narrowing misty funnel of man's
years on earth. There a creature comes shambling into
view: man, man the tool-user, man the fire-maker, man at
last. But he is weak and he is naked; he is really a sorry
thing. His skin is too thin to be much protection, his nails
do poor service as claws, he is wingless, slow of foot, and
vulnerable. Still — he lifts his large head, his brow creased
with perplexity, and he looks up at the stars and listens to
the wind, watches the fire burn, puzzles over the rising
and setting of the sun and the moon. He thinks, he won-

ders, and he dreams. And he learns to tell his thoughts, to pass on his wonderment, to relate the mystery of his dreams to his fellowman.

Birds sing, perhaps even for the sheer joy of it — although we may in saying that be investing birds with humanity — but they do not as individuals improvise songs of varying content and meaning. Dolphins, they say, communicate with each other, but they speak in signals only. A dog may dream of buried bones, a cat of unwary birds, but no dog can tell another dog his bone-filled dreams, and no cat without an amanuensis can write a book.

Other creatures may even appreciate the rest of what man has learned to do. A dog may find contentment in central heating, a cat may be fond of canned tuna or even (we had one such) of television. But though you can, if you wish, tell a story to a cat, he makes a poor critic, and he can never pass your tale on to his kittens.

Only man tells tales of old heroisms and antique infamies, of things long gone or perhaps never to come; only man puts the world inside his skull at the disposal of others. Man alone is a recorder of myths and battles and hopes and fears, a teller and seller of dreams. This is above all the most human of human occupations, the one unshared and unfathomed by any other creature. For all other creatures must eat, sleep, procreate, struggle to live, and in this they share with us a common necessity. Only man tells stories.

But for how long? Alarmed observers of the world of cybernetics point to a day in which machines will write books for us. I believe that there have already been devised methods of programming that will allow a machine to write a horse opera for television. But prefabricated westerns will not throw masses of writers into technological unemployment. A machine can dream only the dreams man feeds to it. Out of what life's riches and disappointments would a computer dream a great novel; from what transistorized griefs and printed-circuit joys and visions could real poetry be programmed to emerge on punch-cards? Lyrics for the popular song, perhaps; or verses for Mother's Day greeting cards, if you're not too fussy about what you say to your mother. But there will never be an electronic Robert Frost capable of writing "The Death of the Hired Man."

When we look back at those rude ancestors of ours, those club wielders and skin wearers, what do we puzzle over most? How they survived? What methods they used to kill their prey? These things we learn as best we can through patient archaeology and scholarly conjecture, but what we puzzle over most and yearn in vain to know is what they dreamed of, what tales they told over their fires, what was inside those suddenly expanded skulls. If only some storyteller, no matter how inept, could have written in those dim days gone, and left us a chronicle from the caves!

So I make no houses and grow no crops, but in my small daily way I am one of man's chroniclers, speaking not only to him but for him, putting on paper a part of his dreams. This most human of human occupations is, after all, central to the identity and uniqueness of man. There is nothing "mere" about it.